CW01501903

For Elaine, my love and the incredible mother to Max;
for Mum, whose memory drives me;
and for Dad – your strength has shaped me –
and my sisters Erica and Leigh, thank you for
always being there

CONTENTS

HEART ON MY SLEEVE

HEART ON MY SLEEVE

My story of struggle and strength

ANDREW PORTER

eriu

First published in the UK in 2025 by Eriu
An imprint of Bonnier Books UK
5th Floor, HYLO, 105 Bunhill Row,
London, EC1Y 8LZ

Copyright © Andrew Porter, 2025

All rights reserved.

No part of this publication may be reproduced, stored or transmitted in
any form or by any means, electronic, mechanical, photocopying or otherwise,
without the prior written permission of the publisher.

The right of Andrew Porter to be identified as Author of this work
has been asserted by him in accordance with the Copyright, Designs and
Patents Act, 1988.

A CIP catalogue record for this book is available from the British Library.

Hardback ISBN: 978-1-80444-264-7

Also available as an ebook and an audiobook

1 3 5 7 9 10 8 6 4 2

Design and Typeset by Envy Design Ltd
Printed and bound in Great Britain by Clays Ltd, Elcograf S.p.A.

Every reasonable effort has been made to trace copyright holders of
material reproduced in this book, but if any have been inadvertently
overlooked the publishers would be glad to hear from them.

This book is a work of Non-Fiction. Some names may have been changed to
respect the privacy of those mentioned.

The authorised representative in the EEA is
Bonnier Books UK (Ireland) Limited.
Registered office address: Floor 3, Block 3, Miesian Plaza,
Dublin 2, D02 Y754, Ireland
compliance@bonnierbooks.ie

www.bonnierbooks.co.uk

Timeline

2008–2014 — Schools Rugby
St Andrew's
College

2014–2016 — All-Ireland League
University College Dublin

2015–2016 — World Rugby U20 Finalist
Ireland U20

2016 — Leinster Debut

2017 — Ireland Senior Debut

2018 — Six Nations Grand Slam
Champions Cup

2022 — Six Nations Triple Crown

2023 — Six Nations Grand Slam

2025 — British and Irish Lions Tour
Australia

FOREWORD

It was Andrew's idea to involve me in interviews for his book, but I still hadn't heard from him. I didn't know the Lions' travel itinerary at the time, but the window was closing fast. He had the URC Final at the end of the week and was due to join up with the Lions in Dublin straight after that. I knew that much, but I didn't know why he hadn't been in touch. And it was starting to concern me. I tried to be open to the possibility that other factors were in play – he had just become a father after all – but he still hadn't contacted me to arrange the first of our meetings.

I had been approached months earlier with a proposal that excited me. Andrew Porter, rather unusually for someone still playing elite sport, intended to write a book. It would feature his rugby career – how could it not –

but it was primarily to be a book about other things. The kind of things that interested me greatly.

He figured a psychotherapist would help him reach the parts of his story that remained hidden, so I was asked would I be up for meeting to chat. There were things he had been through, some of which the public knew about, that he wanted to speak openly about in the book. I was told he wanted to go deeper than he had done previously. I was told he didn't want to skim the surfaces. I liked what I was being told. I agreed instantly to get involved. Months had now passed though, and I still hadn't heard from Andrew.

We weren't arranging therapy sessions, I know, but I approached it as if we were. I decided to text him, which wasn't what I would have wanted. If the therapist is chasing the client, it's not a good start. I figured it didn't bode well for what was to come. All that talk of him being fully committed was at odds with his inaction. Would this be yet another book by a sportsperson that said very little?

We arranged to meet on the Friday, but he cancelled that morning. We rearranged for the Sunday, but yet again, something got in the way. He joined the Lions on Monday, so now we were at the mercy of his schedule. My expectations were lowering fast.

* * *

I first met Andrew at a drinks event in Dublin in September 2022. Equally averse to mingling with the largely unknown crowd around us, we stood together in the corner of the room and made small talk for the evening. He seemed sound. He seemed a decent fella. He wasn't brash in any way. I didn't pick up any superiority complex that often comes with the territory. He just seemed like a really good guy.

Our next meeting was in the Slieve Russell Hotel in Cavan. My role was to interview him in front of a corporate crowd of over 100 guests. By this point, Ireland had been beaten in the World Cup quarter-finals, and Andrew had shared some of his personal story with the media and on the Six Nations documentary on Netflix. What struck me when we spoke over the phone in the run-up was his eagerness and openness to tell his story. Particularly the difficult stuff. Nothing was off the table, he said. You almost never hear that from interviewees before live events.

We agreed to leave space towards the end for Q&A from the crowd. Remarkably, there were as many expressions of gratitude as there were questions. Rather than probe for more detail, many were just thankful for what he said. Hearing someone with Andrew's profile, his career – his appearance – being that open, vulnerable and honest was a new experience for most of the people there. There is power in sharing stories, and Andrew's stories had a remarkable effect on the room.

People approached me afterwards saying how his words had triggered something inside them. They were ready now to take action to help themselves. If someone like Andrew – someone as formidable and fierce as Andrew Porter the rugby player – can talk and act like he did that morning, there was no earthly reason anyone else in the largely male crowd couldn't do the same.

We parted that day with no further plans to meet until the request came earlier this year to chat about the book.

* * *

The first of our conversations finally took place just days before the Lions left for Australia. From the moment he took his seat I knew I had entirely misread the situation to this point. This was not someone from whom I would have to drag details. There would be no need for therapeutic techniques to help me navigate resistance from the person in front of me. Andrew, true to his word from months earlier, was ready to explore the stuff he had never spoken about. And he was determined to do it all for the benefit of this book.

I got to meet young Andrew, the kid going to school trying to deal with the loss of his mum. The grieving child.

I was introduced to Andrew the teenager, completely lost in a world he believed he couldn't survive. One he almost didn't. The aspiring rugby professional emerged somewhere along the way. As did the Ireland international, the loving husband and the doting father.

But it's in his presence where you really appreciate how he's been shaped by it all. He's unavoidably intimidating given his size, but he's equally disarming when he starts to speak candidly about himself. Freakishly strong, yet vulnerable, both tough and kind. A heart the size of his biceps and grounded to boot.

It's not uncommon to hear men speak about mental health anymore or about times when they didn't have all the answers. They can speak honestly about who they are, ignoring what others expect them to be, clearing the path behind them for others to do the same. From the moment I first met him, Andrew spoke candidly and openly, whether in the corner of a crowded room or on the centre of a stage.

I should've known he had good reasons for postponing those initial meetings. I was way off to suspect it revealed a wavering commitment. As he explained when we met over the following weeks, he was simply prioritising the needs of Elaine and their newborn son.

He could've skimmed the surface. He could've left stones unturned. Like the people in the room that day in the Slieve Russell Hotel, I'll be one of the first to say how grateful I am that he didn't.

Congrats on all of it, Ports x

– Richie Sadlier

INTRODUCTION

I'm neither a writer nor a TV personality. I'm a professional sportsperson and I'm much more comfortable on the pitch than in front of a camera. So the idea of taking part in the documentary that then inspired me to write this book came as a bolt from the blue for me.

I'm fairly shy and reserved a lot of the time, but somehow found myself putting my hand up to be in the Netflix documentary *Six Nations: Full Contact*. I took myself by surprise, to be honest, but my wife, Elaine, was very encouraging. 'You need to let people see the other side of you, not just the rugby player who goes out to play on a Saturday.' But what started as a little bit of exposure as a professional sportsperson became something completely different. In the process, it changed my life in many ways.

The series didn't begin brilliantly. In the opening episode, I was filmed tackling Liam Williams late in our match against Wales in the 2023 Six Nations, making myself look pretty stupid in the process. It was a question of mistiming and I was mortified, as you can imagine. I'd cost my team a penalty and no player wants to do that. And they got Lions and England legend Ugo Monye to press the point home on camera! Then, when the camera crew came to Dublin to film me, I wasn't prepared for the depth of the interviews. In professional sport, interactions with the press are quite managed, but this was a lot more personal. I thought, *Wait a minute, I need to gather myself here.* But I didn't want to hold back: I wanted to be authentic and to give a full account of myself and how I've got to where I am now. I needed to be someone different from Andrew Porter the rugby player. After all, what else was I doing it for?

So I found myself answering questions about my mum's death from cancer at the age of 49 when I was twelve, my dad bringing up me and my older sisters Erica and Leigh by himself and my struggles with my mental health, including an eating disorder and thoughts of suicide. I was filmed taking my beloved Old English bulldog, Pablo, for a walk and talking about how hard it is to channel your emotions into the game. I'd never really spoken about my struggles before to anyone other than my closest friends and family, so this was new. I talked about things that I haven't really thought about in years, but I found that it wasn't so bad getting it all out in the open. To use the word 'cathartic' is a bit of a cliché, but it was: I felt that for the first time in my life I was saying 'This is who I am.' I decided that if I was going to tell my story in public like this, there was no way I could present a false version of myself, or not tell the unvarnished truth. When the filming wrapped, I felt a bit lighter, a bit freer, because I'd been fully myself.

Nonetheless, when the documentary came out, I didn't want to watch it. I hate the sound of my own voice and there was no way I was going to enjoy seeing myself on TV, but Elaine, who is always great at pushing me out of my comfort zone, sat me down and said, 'No, you have to watch it.' So I did. And I wasn't totally embarrassed by the way I came across. But more important, I was blown away by the audience reaction. I received hundreds of messages from people telling me how my story had helped them and had made them feel that they weren't alone in their own struggles. What surprised me the most was that a lot of them weren't rugby fans. People from all walks of life were getting in touch with me to tell me that they'd connected with my story. That was a source of particular pride for me.

I suppose that on the outside it might look as if I have it all: I'm successful in my career, I have a close and loving family, I'm fairly well known ... but what people see in the scrum on match day isn't the whole me. There's a side of me that people – even those closest to me – have never seen. It felt great to share that and to hear other people's stories too. I think a lot of people are afraid that if they show any kind of vulnerability, it's a sign of weakness. I'd broken that barrier a few times before, but not in front of a mass audience, and it felt good to take hold of my story, to make sense of it and to connect with other people. We're all scared of what's deep inside us, but if we take even a glimpse at it, it can really make a difference.

I tried to respond to as many messages as I could in person. People had taken the time to reach out and share what they were going through. So many people wrote to me to tell me that they had suffered, or that they had a family member who had been through mental health difficulties and that they could relate to what I was saying. More than that, what I'd said had really helped them. I was blown away by the responses and I wanted to express my gratitude and to support them in return, but there were so many that it wasn't always possible. I felt the responsibility of wanting and needing to, but I'm not the most organised, as you'll discover. To those of you who wrote to me, thank you. Your stories really helped me and I hope that mine helped you too.

I would never say that I'm grateful for what happened in my life, but I know that I wouldn't be me without it. I miss my mum every day. She was my biggest supporter and I can still remember her at my rugby matches when I was a child, cheering me on from the sidelines. I wish she was here to watch me play and, more important, to hold her grandson and to be a source of inspiration and advice. But I am grateful for the love of my dad, Ernie, and Erica and Leigh, Elaine and our son, Max, my old mates from home and school, and my teammates. I've learned to accept that what happened to me has made me the man I am today.

I hope you enjoy reading these reflections on my life and my sport and find something in it, whether you're a rugby head or not. Perhaps you might feel encouraged to move forward in your life, to step outside your own comfort zone, or even just to put one foot in front of the other and keep going. To be who you are. Whatever and whoever you are, thank you for reading this.

Andrew Porter
August 2025

CHAPTER 1

PAYING THE PRICE

'The pain of grief is just as much a part of life as the joy of love; it is, perhaps, the price we pay for love, the cost of commitment.'

Dr Colin Murray Parks, Bereavement: **Studies of Grief in Adult Life (1972)**

The first and really the fundamental loss in my life was that of my mum, Wendy. Every other loss that I've experienced, whether on the field or in life, comes back to that. When she died, after a long struggle with cancer, I lost her, but I also lost my family, as we each grieved in our own way. People often say that grief can bring a family together, but in our case, we were all in our own worlds, trying to make sense of it in our own different ways. Now, we're a close family, but back then it was incredibly hard.

I remember starting secondary school the day after my mother's funeral. I suppose they thought it would be a good distraction for me and I'd need to start school sooner or later, but I wasn't a bit happy when Dad drove me to the gates because I just didn't want to be there. He gave me a hug and urged me out of the car, but my feet felt like lead. I had no desire to be in this strange place. I'd gone to primary school in tiny St Brigid's in Stillorgan, so St Andrew's in Booterstown, with more than one thousand students and two hundred staff, felt huge by comparison. My cousin David was in the year above me and my friend from primary school Andrew Meates was in another form, but quite honestly I would have felt lonely even if my family had come in and sat in the classroom with me. My mum had just died and life was continuing as normal. I just didn't understand.

I can't remember if anyone said anything to me about Mum. My form teacher, Mr Conaty, definitely knew my situation and kept an eye out for me, and I did settle down and make friends in the end. My home economics buddy, Alasdair Murphy, is still a good friend: we bonded over making shepherd's pie in first year. But the years that followed were dark ones, as I struggled to deal with the usual teenage stuff as well as grieving the loss of my mum.

I didn't do a great job of it. I thought I could work it all out on my own: I was wrong. I've had to learn the hard way that bottling up your feelings doesn't make them go away. In my case, it just made me more determined to push them down, and that caused me a lot of problems. I needed other people, I know that now. Sometimes I think it's an irony that I chose a sport in which the players are so close-knit that they've become family. Rugby was, and still is, the place in which I feel fully myself.

I've done a lot of reading over the years, to come to terms with loss and losing, and to control a mind that sometimes seems to run away from me. Structure is incredibly important to me, as is both physical and mental training. I've also read the journals of Marcus Aurelius, the last great emperor of Rome and one of the earliest Stoic philosophers. In spite of the fact that he wrote his thoughts down two thousand years ago, to me they're incredibly relevant today. His *Meditations* is full of wise advice and he has taught me a lot about life. One of his ideas concerns the principle of loving our fate. Whatever happens to us, whether it's positive or negative, we have to love it, because that's what moulds us as people. How you react to situations is how you carry yourself as a person. You have no control over outside events or what other people do to you or think about you, but you have full control over your reaction to situations.

If someone says something about you, and you want to be offended or harmed by it, that's your choice. It's not about ignorance or passivity but acceptance. Acceptance, to me, is what really matters. As Marcus Aurelius said, 'You have power over your mind – not outside events.

Realise this, and you will find strength.' Lesson number one! I have tried to apply this lesson to my life every day.

I also find that Ryan Holiday's books, such as *The Obstacle is the Way*, and his Daily Stoic newsletter full of interesting and worthwhile advice, can make a big difference to the way I see things. What is meant by 'the obstacle is the way' is that life is rarely easy, so we need to embrace that difficulty and go through it to come out the other side better and stronger. I find that essential both on the pitch and in life.

The quarter-finals of the Rugby World Cup in Paris in 2023 is a very good example of this philosophy in action. Losing to the All Blacks was crushing. I can still remember the last few minutes of the match: we had nothing left in the tank, and those last 37 phases to get the ball up to the New Zealand 22-metre line took everything we had. It wasn't enough. We were devastated. Sure, we'd been beaten by a great team, who had the help of master tactician Joe Schmidt, who knew us better than anyone, but as the world's number one team, expectations had been high – and we expected a lot of ourselves. I know that Johnny Sexton said that we 'couldn't have done more', and that we hadn't got our fairy-tale ending, but it felt like small consolation to me. I knew that I *could* have done more. Especially in the front row there is that added pressure, a responsibility on you when a decision that doesn't go your way can tip things in favour of the opposition. I had given away a few penalties in the game and I suppose I lost the head a small bit. It was the sheer frustration of not being able to make a breakthrough and that a few decisions had gone against me.

I felt that the mistakes I made in the game had cost us the result. The stakes were so high. We'd all desperately wanted to win the game for Johnny as it was his last tournament for Ireland, to send him off on a high. I felt I'd let him down. I felt I'd let everyone down: my family; my friends, who were all in the stands looking on; and particularly the fans. In the six weeks we'd been in France, it seemed that the whole country was behind us. Nobody needed to remind me that it was our eighth quarter-final loss.

I have never felt that much of a low in my career. There had been huge hype and huge expectation. So many Irish fans travelled over and there was this unbelievable, special atmosphere at the games that I've never witnessed before. All that linked together, building up expectations, and it's like a rollercoaster, and then – bang, you're at the bottom.

I played in the Junior World Championship in 2015 and 2016, and two World Cup tournaments for Ireland at senior level. Unfortunately the outcome has been the same, but on each occasion we thought we'd done everything we possibly could.

Of course, I had followed Ireland's progress in tournaments as a kid, particularly when we lost to Wales in the quarter-finals in Wellington in 2011. I can still remember feeling Brian O'Driscoll's disappointment as my own. We'd beaten Australia convincingly in the group stages only to go out against our neighbours. It was devastating, even if Brian said stoically afterwards that we'd simply have to suck it up. He was right. There's not a lot else you can do. Then there was 2015, when Argentina ended our hopes of victory. Arguably it was an incredibly tough match against France the week before that really did the damage, with so many injuries in the squad, including Peter O'Mahony, Johnny Sexton and Paul O'Connell. The lads who replaced them were valiant, but it was always going to be tough to beat the Pumas.

My very first World Cup was 2019 in Japan, and I was a sub for Tadhg Furlong at tighthead. I was versatile and could play at both tighthead and loosehead prop, and I was determined to make the biggest impact that I could off the bench. I'd never thought I'd have the opportunity to visit Japan and it was an amazing experience. When I went to the swimming pool I had to cover my tattoos with these odd-looking sleeves and stockings, because of the association of tattoos with the Yakuza crime gangs in Japan, and I also missed out on a trip to the *onsen* (public sauna) because of them, but it didn't matter. I loved the people and the place and the food was delicious. I became a big fan of sushi and ramen. It was all the more special because Dad travelled over to watch me and it was fantastic to have him there, even if he couldn't manage the food …

We beat Scotland comfortably in the first game, before losing 19–12 to Japan a week later in the Shizuoka Stadium in Fukuroi. The Japanese were truly outstanding in that match. Full of pace and spurred on by the home crowd, their attacking game forced us into defensive errors. I think Michael Morrow of the BBC hit the nail on the head when he said, 'This was not a result borne of Irish indiscipline or stage fright, but of a truly stunning Japanese performance in front of a cacophonous crowd that lifted their side with a stunning noise that greeted every metre gained, tackle made and turnover won.' It's amazing what the fans can do to lift a side – we've experienced it ourselves – but the Japanese were the better team on the day.

Thankfully two wins over Russia and Samoa saw us into the quarter-final against New Zealand. It was the seventh time Ireland had reached the quarter-finals.

We'd already proved in autumn 2018 that we could beat the mighty All Blacks – and we've gone on to do so since – but maybe we'd run out of steam by the time the World Cup came around. The All Blacks wreaked their revenge on us in the quarter-finals in Tokyo, beating us 46–14 in what was to be Rory Best's last game in the green jersey and Joe Schmidt's last outing as our head coach. It wasn't a pleasant feeling.

That's a lot of baggage for any team to carry, but 2023 was going to be our year. We were the number one team in the world, according to the world rankings. I can't say that I understand the whole ranking system, but because of our status there was, from the outside, an expectation that we'd just go in and win it. We'd had a great Six Nations season after winning the Grand Slam, so there was a lot of expectation because of our form.

We knew exactly how tough the World Cup was and there was no complacency in the squad going into the tournament. In big games, small things matter: little mistakes can cost you the game. Also, playing four games in five weeks at group stage is exciting but pretty demanding. There are no easy games in the World Cup: each game takes its toll in a different way and each team is different, but what they all have in common is their calibre. We're playing at the highest level. Yes, we were confident in our abilities and in our connectedness as a team, and we knew that the combination we had worked really well, but we weren't in any way complacent.

I think some of the noise is sometimes projected onto

us as a team. I remember in the recent Six Nations, some pundit said that Ireland could beat Wales with thirteen men, and it turned out that Wales ran us very close that time, because they played really well. And then, of course, we read about our own arrogance in thinking we could beat Wales with thirteen men, etc. It's all a lot of fluff, really, talking us up before a match or tournament, but it rarely reflects the way we're feeling. So, in France, the notion in the media that we had every chance to win it was taken by other countries as arrogance – the Irish team is saying they can win. We had their backs up before the tournament started.

One thing that stood out in the lead-up to the tournament was that Andy Farrell, the Ireland coach, invited Ireland and Lions greats Brian O'Driscoll and David Irwin to talk to us. It was incredibly emotional. For us youngsters, born at around the time of the Good Friday Agreement, the Troubles were an historical event; grainy pictures of bombings in Belfast and Derry, British soldiers on street corners, guns at the ready. It was all a very long time ago. So it was a revelation to hear what David, in particular, had to say. I hadn't understood the significance of what he'd gone through during the Troubles simply to play the game he loved until I saw the documentary made by Brian O'Driscoll and Craig Doyle on the history behind the song 'Ireland's Call'. I was really moved by his account of an incident that he and his fellow players Philip Rainey and Nigel Carr were caught up in. They had been heading south for training for the first rugby World Cup in 1987 when on a small country road near the border, an IRA car bomb intended for a senior judge and his wife exploded. The judge, Maurice Gibson, and his wife were both killed, and the players, who had been travelling in the other direction, were caught in the blast. David and Philip Rainey sustained minor injuries, but Nigel Carr broke a lot of bones and would miss the World Cup. I couldn't imagine what it would be like to go through that just to play for my country. Let's just say, I belted out 'Ireland's Call' at the France match that Saturday, understanding its significance fully for the first time. The fact that rugby is a 32-county sport in Ireland is something we should be proud of.

There was such a lot of energy around the team in Tours, in the centre of France, which was our base for the tournament, and a lot of excitement in France in general. A personal highlight for me was visiting a children's cancer centre in the city along with Bundee Aki, Mack Hansen, Joe McCarthy and Mick Kearney. The kids were amazing, so full of energy as they added to my tattoo collection in marker pen. We threw a ball around with them and had a lot of fun. Their bravery was exceptional and it really moved me; we meet so many people when we're on tour, but this visit was one I won't forget.

However, as our pool contained South Africa, Tonga, Scotland and Romania we knew that we were up against it. Our first game against Romania in Bordeaux helped to settle us. We scored twelve tries and had a comprehensive 82–8 win, but it showed up our weaknesses too – basic errors like losing lineouts and getting turned over. We couldn't let that happen next time.

The game against the reigning champions, South Africa, was to be held in the iconic Stade de France in Paris and, of course, we were keyed up. It was one of the most anticipated matches of the tournament and promised to be 'as tight as a facelift', as one commentator put it. At this point, I had made the shift to loosehead – Tadhg Furlong was tighthead. That night in Paris was one of the most physical games I've ever played. South Africa came at us with everything. Their pack was massive, their bench even bigger, and every collision felt like a car crash. We knew it would be a battle of inches. I remember the first scrum. We held firm, then got a nudge. That gave us belief. Bundee was immense in defence and Hugo Keenan was flawless under the high ball. I carried hard, tried to win the gain line and hit every ruck like it was my last. We went in at half-time ahead but knew they'd come back. They did. It was 13–8 with ten minutes to go. We had to dig deep. I remember one defensive set on our line where we made five tackles in a row. When the final whistle went, I was on my knees. Exhausted. Elated. We'd beaten the world champions. The crowd was incredible. Green everywhere. That win felt like a statement. We were here to do more than compete. We were here to win.

I can remember the *Irish Independent* describing my game afterwards: 'Enjoyed a real battle come scrum-time, getting done in the build-up to South Africa's try but earned the penalty out of Malherbe that gave Ireland the lead on the hour. 75 minutes was a phenomenal effort.' I felt every one of those 75 minutes. The scoreline reflected just how tough a match it had been.

Tonga really tested us too, they pushed us hard to the end of the match. They really were physical, especially in the breakdown early on, but we won most of the lineouts and Johnny was in amazing form on the day where he overtook Ronan O'Gara's international points record for Ireland, reaching 1,090 points in the game. I had an opening try ruled out by the television match official (TMO), but we still scored a flurry of tries just before half-time through Caelan Doris, Mack Hansen and Garry Ringrose. Those scores dented the Tongans' confidence, but they bounced back well and scored a try through Vaea Fifita, who put in an amazing performance. William Havili, the New Zealand-born Tonga international, took the conversion, and also scored three penalties. We knew that Tonga were tiring because of the sheer energy they had put into their attack, but we continued to control the territory and kept the pressure on, resulting in a bonus point win. It was a really exciting game of rugby.

And then came the quarter-final and the rest, as they say, is history.

CHAPTER 2

THE REST IS HISTORY

'It is not death that a man should fear, but he should
fear never beginning to live.'

Marcus Aurelius, Meditations

No excuses from any one of us. The worst thing was that after six weeks of fantastic play, we went home the day after our match and that was it. We'd spent practically every waking moment together during the tournament; we'd done so much pre-season work. We were family. And then we all dispersed. We had a small meeting during which Andy Farrell offered us some words of consolation, and then we were gone. I came home and Elaine didn't really know what to say to me. How do you console someone who, in his mind, is responsible for such a loss? There's not a lot you can say.

For me, the whole thing was probably compounded by the fact that there had been a lot going on for me in the background during the tournament. I'd lost my granny in Dublin, whom I was very close to. Granny Joan had been in a nursing home for a little while due to dementia, but she'd been a fantastic hockey player, a talent that she'd passed on to Mum and to my sister Erica. Because we were mid-tournament, I didn't get to go home for her funeral, so I watched it on Zoom and felt as if everyone was a million miles away. My sister Leigh also lost a friend to suicide and I wished I could have been there to talk to her and to offer my support. However, as a professional, I knew that I had to park all this while I was playing – we all do that. Gary Keegan, our mental skills coach, makes sure that we prepare well mentally as well as physically for each match. You have to bring yourself to that dark place in your mind where you know you are going to have to get through a lot of work, but you take a lot of confidence from the guys either side of you, that they've been able to get through so much work. We block out anything that isn't relevant to that one match. If you are on top of everything mentally, it makes the physical side of things easier. At the same time, everyone has something going on in their life. I did park it, but after the tournament, it really hit me.

At first, distraction came in the form of a delayed honeymoon, ten days in New York. It was fantastic, actually. We'd got married earlier that summer during a week off from pre-season training, which in itself was a feat of organisation. Rugby has such a tough schedule, and it changes all the time. I think seven of us got married in the same week! Now Elaine and I had time to take that much-needed break. New York was just the job – it was loud and exciting enough to completely distract me from the World Cup comedown – and what was even better was that, apart from a few Irish guys who came up to say hello, no one knew who I was. I felt that Elaine and I were in a bubble of shopping and sightseeing, far away from reality.

Of course, when I came home, all the feelings I'd suppressed came back to me. It felt like a form of sleep paralysis, where you wake up at night constantly thinking there's something lurking in the corner of the bedroom. A shadow that I couldn't grasp. I became a hermit, I suppose. I just didn't want to talk to anyone, particularly my teammates, because I felt like I'd let them down. I was really struggling being at home after being in such a great environment with all those incredibly special people, players and coaches, for so long.

Looking back, I realise that, after all, it's a team sport. There are obviously so many things going on in the game that winning or losing is never really down to one player. It's the nature of any sport – you win and you lose, and that's the beauty of it – but the highs are incredibly high and the lows incredibly low. At the time, I suppose I was just really hard on myself. People would come up to me in the supermarket to commiserate and to tell me how gutted they were for all of us and that was so welcome, but it felt as if I'd let the country down as well. Johnny had been right: we'd wanted the fairy-tale ending so badly that when it didn't happen, it hurt all the more.

In the weeks that followed I had more than enough time to think about my mistakes. I'd be up at night, over-analysing every move of the match, replaying it in my head, knowing that I could have done better. There was nothing I could do to change the past, so I moped around beating myself up for my mistakes when I couldn't do anything about them. I know that my thinking was flawed but my self-esteem had taken such a blow that I couldn't think about the bigger picture: it was all my mistakes, my fault. Thinking about it now, I remember telling David Walsh of *The Times* about losing to Saracens in the 2020 European Cup quarter-final, 'I find it very easy to blame myself for things that go wrong. That's something I'm particularly bad at. A bad defeat can take over your personal life because you're constantly thinking about it. After that Saracens loss I went for countless drives by myself to play music. I could be gone for two hours. I'd park up somewhere, just try to process it. Sometimes it works. Sometimes it doesn't.

I'll always suffer from that, but I'd like to shift the balance a little bit, take less of it on myself.' I'm not sure if I've succeeded, but I've consciously tried.

Looking back, I can see that I had to go through that experience so that I could reach out and ask for help. I've always tried to solve any problems myself: I'd say, 'This is my problem and I can work it out', but I couldn't. I really envied Elaine her women friends, because they could all talk it out – we men tend to keep our feelings to ourselves and it's lonely. So I decided to talk to a therapist about it. I knew that it wasn't a problem that I could solve myself. I needed to take a broader perspective and to get to the bottom of why I was feeling the way I was feeling. I wanted to understand more about myself and my thought process.

We have a brilliant sports psychologist on the Ireland team, who has done incredible work with me recently, but I really wanted to talk to someone outside the game to give me that big-picture perspective. I wanted to be the best player I could be and I knew that I couldn't just rely on my body; so much of the game is mental, so I wanted to gain a deeper understanding of that side of things. Why was I feeling the way I was feeling and how could I overcome this psychological hurdle?

My therapist was a great help to me in putting the

whole thing in perspective. She helped me to realise that I was making the defeat into something it wasn't. Instead of understanding that I'd simply made mistakes, I was thinking that I was the worst player ever. I was thinking, *Is this job really for me? Am I really any good at this?* There's so much self-doubt, I suppose.

But then something the therapist said really made sense to me. She said that when you have lost someone close to you and you have another loss, your mind goes straight back to the first; it's like muscle memory – you think that that's how loss should feel. Maybe that's why my reaction to our World Cup defeat had been so dramatic. It was a double-edged sword in that nothing could compare to that first loss of Mum, but at the same time, I was experiencing every loss after it like the first.

I started thinking about that and remembering. Memories of my mum always involve her laughing and relaxing in Brittas Bay with her siblings and their children. Together with her brother, she'd bought what was basically a tin shack in a field near the beach. This they called 'The Nook'. It was made of corrugated steel, so it was boiling in the summer and freezing in the winter. It had concrete floors and we kids all slept upstairs in the attic. It was also a really odd shape, like a chevron. It has since been rebuilt, but it's kept that distinctive shape.

It's incredibly special to me because it's where I remember Mum the most vividly, shooing us out the door to run around in the fields and scoot around on our bikes until we got hungry and came in again, as well as giving out to me for whatever scrape I'd got myself into. 'Leave your sisters alone,' was a common refrain. I spent a lot of my childhood trying to annoy them. Evenings would be spent over an improvised bonfire in the back garden, which had been built in the drum of a washing machine and where we'd toast marshmallows and Mum would try to stop me going too near the flames. Mum also loved swimming and I can remember her teaching me to swim, me kicking furiously in the swimming pool as she held my hands, or splashing around with us on the beach.

I also loved Christmas with Granny, Mum's step-mother, in Dundrum, when all fifteen of us cousins and various other relatives would squeeze into her house to exchange presents and eat sausage rolls, my cousin David and I tackling each other in the garden. David and I were best friends growing up, getting into mischief together. One of our biggest pranks was going around the neighbourhood at Hallowe'en stuffing the pumpkins on people's doorsteps with fireworks to make them explode. The gardaí were called that time, so we settled for less ambitious pranks after that. David lives in Brisbane now, but even though we're on opposite sides of the world, we'll always be best mates.

Mum was such an amazing mum. After she died, I found it really hard to enjoy Christmas, even though everyone was trying their best to make things festive. I actually hated it for a bit, because it reminded me of what we were missing. You always think about the person you love and miss on special occasions and wish they were there to share them. When I look at photos of Mum with us when we were children, it brings her back to me so clearly. I can see the beam of pride on her face, can feel her giving me a hug. Of course, she is still with me in spirit, I know that, but as I grow older, it's harder to hang on to memories of her. I remember really struggling to recall her voice at one point, so one of my sisters found an old recording of Mum and put it onto a USB stick for me. The minute I heard her voice, she came back to me as if it were yesterday. I can hear her cheering me on in matches and she becomes a real person for me again.

Bringing Elaine down to Brittas for the first time meant a lot. There are pictures of Mum everywhere with us as children and it felt as if she was getting to know a part of me and getting to know my mum as well.

To this day, people will come up to me and share memories of Mum. When I was in Portugal at the Irish training camp for the World Cup, Denis O'Brien paid a visit and he told me that he remembered Mum well. She had shown him around on his very first day at work in the bank, and she'd been lovely, he said. It's incredible to see how many people remember her smile, her kindness, her light-heartedness. She was the very first person I confided my childhood dream in: that I wanted to become a professional rugby player. Her response was typical of her: she was delighted. She encouraged me to believe that with hard work, anything is possible. I wish she'd been able to see me play. All the matches, the caps, the Grand Slam wins, she is there in spirit, but I would give anything to have her on the sidelines cheering me on. Mum taught me the importance of respecting other people, of being friendly and polite, interested in everyone, just like her. I really treasure those values.

I don't know if I have a real sense of when Mum became ill, because I was only six or so and because I spent such a lot of time on my uncle's farm in Carlow. I'm sure that Dad would have told me about her illness in a way I could understand, but somehow I can't get to that memory. I'm not sure if I've blocked it out or simply can't remember, but from talking to my sisters about it, it's clear they were a lot more aware of what was happening.

I can remember the day Mum died, however. At this

stage, she was in Blackrock Hospice. I can still remember how peaceful it was, as if the spirit of the Carmelite nuns who'd once lived there still lingered. Whenever I'd visited before, she'd been asleep. I wasn't sure if I should wake her, or if she could hear me when I said 'Mum'. I remember wanting to tell her about what I was doing but not being sure if she'd be able to hear me. I remember listening to her breathing, which seemed to be slow and shallow, and breathing in time with her. Was she still Mum if she couldn't see and hear me or hug me, or laugh at one of my schoolboy jokes?

She died on 22 August 2008. What I remember of the day is that I was heading out to play with my friends, because the summer holidays were almost over. My school uniform was hanging in my bedroom wardrobe, ready for me to put on and to begin my brand-new life in secondary school. Meanwhile, we had a few precious days left and I'm sure an elaborate game of soccer was planned on the green. Just as I was leaving, Dad took me to one side. 'We're going to visit your mum,' he said gently. Okay, I thought, getting ready to hop into the car and make the journey to the hospice. We visited Mum regularly and I expected this to be another trip to see her asleep in bed while we sat around her and talked in whispers.

This time, when we entered Mum's room, it was filled

with family members. I can remember thinking, *What's everyone doing here?* I don't recall understanding that Mum was close to the end at this point, even looking at everyone's faces, feeling the pats on the shoulder, the gentle questions about my summer. Yet she must have been. Now, I wish I had said something to her, because I'd never get the chance again.

I wore my brand-new school uniform for the funeral, my navy blue jumper with the St Andrew's crest on it, blue tie, grey trousers and black shoes. The procession of cars up to Taney church was endless and the church was so packed that people spilled out of the doors into the car park. I can remember that we needed a police escort for the trip to Mount Jerome Crematorium. The night before, we had gathered in the funeral home in Dundrum to say our goodbyes. I can remember clearly hovering near the back of the room, watching everyone walk up to Mum's coffin, and yet my feet were rooted to the spot. I couldn't do it. I couldn't walk up to her and look at her and say something, because I didn't know what to say. I didn't have the words. That person wasn't my mum as I remembered her.

In the years after Mum's death, I would find it hard to forgive myself for that. That I hadn't said goodbye to her. Everyone told me that it was fine: Dad, my sisters, friends, but I knew that it wasn't. I carried that guilt with me for a long time and I know that it affected me in so many ways. I often think that how I react to losses stems directly from that first loss.

It took me many years – and my fantastic therapist – to understand that nothing on the field actually compares to losing Mum. Compared to that loss, it's just a game. We're like gladiators in the Colosseum, a distraction for people watching us, a unifying experience around which there's a lot of chatter and noise. But the next day, people get up and they go about their daily lives and they're not thinking about me, or about the Ireland team, or about the mistakes they have or haven't made. Liverpool manager Bill Shankly once said about soccer, 'Somebody said that football's a matter of life and death to you. I said, "Listen, it's more important than that."' I disagree. Nothing is more important than family and loved ones. After talking to the therapist, I understood that perhaps I'd always come back to that first loss; it would be a touchstone for me for the rest of my life. There was no outrunning it, but I could understand that other losses just didn't compare.

And so, I began to relax a bit. I met up with a few of my old friends and, over a few pints, I realised that they were dealing with their issues too. Everyone has problems. Everyone is fighting his or her own battles. Besides, they cut me nicely down to size! To them, I wasn't Andrew

Porter, loosehead prop for Ireland, I was just a person. I was just me, the guy they'd always hung around with in school, or in Cabinteely Park, the guy they'd always slagged. With them, I was able to step away from rugby for a bit, and realise that in the grand scheme of things, it was no more important than anything else.

In November I went back to training with my Leinster teammates and we just started again. I realised that I could work on everything and improve, mentally and physically. There was a sense of continuity for me, of being able to keep going and keep working to improve my performance. It's the nature of sport that you're going to lose, but you have to learn to take it on the chin and pick yourself up and come back stronger. It's tough because even at Leinster, we've got to a few finals over the last few years and then come up short in the end – all we could do until we won the United Rugby Championship in June 2025 was to keep going.

I had a new perspective on the World Cup loss, too. We may not have beaten our quarter-final curse, but one day we would. And we'd lost to a great team: they were worthy winners of that match. Over time, I felt the weight lift off my shoulders. I had been holding on to the loss and now, slowly, I could let it go. I could stop thinking about what I didn't have – a win – and start thinking about what I did have. My dad, who kept checking in on me; my sisters; Elaine, who was always there for me; my friends; and, eventually, the excitement of expecting a baby. I could also understand more of my feelings around loss and why I took it so much to heart. All along, my family had been there for me and now, I could see that. Even though Mum isn't there to cheer me on, Dad is – so many people still are. My teammates, my family, my coaches, my schoolmates. Everyone just wanted the best for me: I could see that now and look forward to the future instead of looking back at the past.

CHAPTER 3

THIS IS WHO I AM

'Nothing happens to anybody which he is not
fitted by his own nature to bear. Shame on the soul,
to falter on the road of life while the body
still perseveres.'

Marcus Aurelius, **Meditations**

'I'm sorry, you're just not big enough.'

It was 2012 and I was standing in front of the Leinster under-16s coach, John Fogarty, head hanging. The disappointment was crushing. I thought that the trials for the team had gone well. I'd given it my all in my position and thought that I'd given a good account of myself. Worse than being knocked back, for me, was that I couldn't control my emotions. It was clear to John that I was really upset about it and in spite of him trying to soften the blow with encouragement, it was hard not to show him how devastated I was. I'd worked so hard for this, building myself up physically and eating well, so to find that, irony of ironies, I wasn't big enough was gutting.

I slunk off the pitch to the dressing room to lick my wounds. For a while, I looked blankly at the grubby rubber matting of the changing-room floor, negative thoughts chasing through my head. *You're not up to it. You'll never make the grade. You're just not good enough for national rugby.* I let my thoughts circle for a bit, agreeing that yes, I wasn't up to the job and that I'd been hard done by, but then I made a decision: no one would ever tell me that I wasn't big enough again. After everything I'd been through over the past four years or so, I wasn't going to give in. Not now. And so I set about the task of showing John – showing myself – what I was really capable of.

When you get criticism, no matter how positive it might be, it's easy to let it get to you. In *Six Nations: Full Contact*, John Fogarty – Foggy, as we call him – said that he could see how devastated I was at his assessment and that he wanted to look out for me because of that. (By now, John was Ireland's scrum coach.) I was gutted at the time, because when someone puts the problem out there clearly, and doesn't beat around the bush about it, it's tough. At the same time, though, it makes the goal clearer. So when John said, 'I'm sorry, you're just not big enough,' I was almost embarrassed that he'd said it to me. I knew that I still wasn't the best rugby player, but it was the size issue that got to me. I'd gone from being the biggest kid in the class to the smallest, then had done everything in my power to make myself bigger. I took the criticism to heart. But I also thought, *So that's what I need to do. That's what I need to go after.* I was determined to get myself to a place where no one could say that to me again. That's what took me to 131 kg in 2016. With John's words in my mind, I worked hard and ate even harder to make that weight.

Nowadays, a lot is made of the fact that I can lift 325 kg, but it wasn't always like that. I wasn't always as confident about my body and what it could do: quite the opposite. From way back in childhood, I was really self-conscious about it, so accepting who I am has been a long and challenging process.

To put it bluntly, I was the fat kid in the class in primary school and I was teased accordingly. And being a big guy, I took everyone on. I wasn't violent or a bully, but if I was attacked I'd fight back. I was an angry kid and hadn't yet found an outlet for that anger. I think a lot of it came from the fact that I couldn't articulate my feelings very well. 'Use your words,' the teacher might say to me, but I just couldn't. I think that contributed to the anger I felt.

My mum was called into the school regularly and I can still remember the look she'd give me when she received a call from my teacher. Here we go again, it said. I had friends but quite honestly, I spent a lot of time in a classroom on my own. Later, I would learn just why I was disruptive in the classroom, but at that stage, all I knew was that I couldn't help myself. The very idea of sitting down in one place and paying attention was a mystery to me, as was joining in with the class activities and listening to my teacher.

My outlet was mini rugby, which I started in my dad's club, Old Wesley, aged four. Here, my size wasn't an issue, because I would play with the kids at the next level up from mine, along with my cousin David. But off the field, I just wanted to fit in. And fitting in meant being a normal size.

I can still remember going to the pharmacy with my mum – so I must have been quite young – and while she was at the counter, I scanned the shelves of diet products. I examined the boxes full of packets promising instant weight loss, with 'for adults only' written in bold type across the front. Not seeing what I wanted, I went up to the pharmacist. 'Excuse me? Do you have any weight-loss supplements for children?'

I can't remember if Mum said anything – I'm sure she did – but the pharmacist looked taken aback, and then said, 'If you just eat healthily and exercise, you'll be fine.' I didn't really believe him, or the adults who told me that it was just puppy fat and I'd lose it when I got a bit older. I didn't want to wait until I was older. I wanted to be normal right now. The only place where I was free of my self-consciousness was on the rugby field. I was fast for my size and it never prevented me from playing, so I looked forward to minis, because then I could speed up the field or put my full strength into a scrum and not feel that I was going to flatten someone. And it was a great outlet for the anger. I could channel it, discipline it into the game.

My eating disorder crept up on me. It wasn't as if my parents said anything: my dad was a big man and had played rugby for Kilkenny College, Carlow and Old Wesley – in fact, many of his contemporaries would tell me they used to dread him, because in spite of his size, he was a back, so he'd be running over the top to destroy you. I idolised my dad and wanted to eat dad-sized portions of food, but I was merely a schoolboy with a big appetite. Mum had a completely normal attitude towards food, but somehow I'd internalised this idea that in order to fit in, I had to shrink myself, physically and mentally.

I didn't understand it at the time, but Mum's illness was always present in my young life. She became ill with breast cancer when I was about six. I know that I was aware of it, but at that age, I couldn't really understand what was going on. My sisters were a bit older than me, so they had a much greater awareness of what was happening. I do remember her explaining chemotherapy to me and telling me that her hair would probably fall out: all I can remember is that she wore a wig and would often let me try it on. I suspect that one part of me thought that it was some sort of game.

The other part was trying to absorb the information that my mother had something very wrong with her and I didn't understand what that was. So, when I try to disentangle my issues with food from Mum's illness, I find it hard.

It was after Mum's death that I became really regimented about my food intake. Actually, that's an understatement: I slowly stopped eating. With my dad out at work, earning a living to raise us all as well as grieving, and my two sisters in secondary school, it wasn't hard to slip under the radar. I'd eat nothing for breakfast, then avoid eating lunch in school, which wasn't difficult – I could always make up a story about having forgotten my lunch – and when it came to dinner, I'd make an excuse about having eaten earlier before training. That, or I'd eat, then quietly go upstairs and throw up. I became obsessive about eating as little as I needed to survive. If I was offered an apple, I'd nibble on the skin and leave the rest.

I'm sure people knew that I wasn't eating properly but didn't know what to do about it. My dad, who would have done anything for me and did the best he could, didn't have the words to deal with an illness like this, and in a young boy at that. Eating disorders are such an insidious thing: you almost don't see them creeping up on you, but before you know it, you become accustomed to not eating, to not feeling hungry. To letting an entire day pass without thinking about food. The only thing I could think about was that I had it all under control. And having something I was in charge of was essential in a life that was spinning rapidly out of control. I was lost, angry and missed my mum more than I thought was possible. Her death, like any death from cancer, was traumatic, and I couldn't talk about any of it.

How I managed to train as hard as I did after school is a mystery to me. I do have one photo of me taken at a Wesley rugby camp in Biarritz. I think I was around thirteen, but I look younger. Of course, I was skinny – we all were at that stage, getting longer, not wider – but I have a drawn look on my face and when I look at my younger self, it makes me want to cry. The rest of the lads used to joke that Porter was always asleep on the team bus, probably as a result of not eating. In fact I'd nod off anywhere: once, in Biarritz, we were watching the 2009 Lions tour to South Africa, which I wouldn't have missed for the world, and there I was, snoozing away in the corner.

Of course, I didn't have the energy to live, not to mention play a game that relies so much on physical energy, but I was too young and too scared to express what I was feeling and so I turned it inwards. Those first few years in secondary school were incredibly tough. I wasn't present. Second year was the worst. In spite of myself, I had managed to make friends, and they knew that there was something wrong with my eating, but it was a kind of unspoken secret between us. What I didn't doubt, though, was the fact that they were all there for me. They still are. I didn't really get into trouble, because I didn't really act out: I was late a few times, and got detention, but I was more of a withdrawn kid, there but not there.

The only place where I felt real was on the rugby pitch. It was where I could truly be myself. I could completely live in the moment and it was a form of meditation to me. The rituals of putting on the kit, walking out onto the pitch in all weathers, taking up my position, listening to the coach, doing what I knew I needed to do and when I needed to do it – it all really helped me. Without it, I don't know what would have happened to me. I suppose it's an irony that I went to St Andrew's, not renowned as a rugby school. In my year, though, there were a few of us who were capable: myself, Johnny Guy, Jordan Larmour, Greg Jones, so maybe it was a good thing in that, ultimately, it would be easier to stand out.

My saviour was a man called David Jones, our PE teacher and rugby coach. He was scary: he'd done mixed martial arts way before it was a thing and he was really into strength and conditioning – nowadays, that's probably what he'd be doing professionally, but he was ahead of his time. Some of us used to dread him, but I thought he was great. He understood that there was something going on for me and he really took me under his wing in school. He was the first person to teach me that what you put in is what you get out. Mr Jones emphasised the value of hard work, of proper training and nutrition and the safest ways to build strength. In fact, he was the first person to really help me become aware of the fact that more than talent, it's hard work that sets elite athletes apart. I really believe this. I don't think that my talent as a schoolboy was greater than many others' but a combination of my family's work ethic and sheer determination helped to make me into a professional. More important, it made me someone who could take knock-backs and come back stronger.

There were two turning points in my struggles with food. First, Mr Jones took me to one side after training one day and handed me an Irish Rugby Football Union (IRFU) leaflet on nutrition for young players. I read it many times and looked at the information on what a player needs to eat to fuel their game, the input of proteins, fats and carbs, their balance, and something clicked. The IRFU logo was impressive, I thought. If they were saying this, there must be some truth to it. I began to examine nutrition carefully, to read up as much as I could on the subject. By the end of second year, going on into third year, I slowly began to give myself permission to eat more, telling myself that it was to fuel my training. That way, I could accept something that had really been difficult for me up to that point.

The second turning point was watching my cousin Rob at home on the farm in Clonegal eat his dinner! It must have been some time in 2010, because I was still conscious about what I was eating. I wasn't fully over my issues with food. I was hyper aware of what I was eating the whole time, telling myself what I could and couldn't eat, what was permitted and what was forbidden. I went down to the farm for the summer, as I'd done pretty much every summer since childhood. My cousin Rob was my idol at the time. He was a bit older than me, a really big guy who worked hard on the farm and who played rugby for Tullow RFC. As a result he ate all around him. He had a healthy appetite, because he was fuelling a day's hard work and an evening's training. I can still remember watching him eat in the kitchen one day and thinking, *Oh, he's just eating that big dinner and he's not thinking about it.* He's not examining every bite, he's not pushing it around on his plate, he's not disguising his intake by hiding the food, he's just … eating. Another penny dropped. That in order to emulate the cousin who was my idol, and to become a professional rugby player, I'd need to eat.

Of course, I'm simplifying a complicated disease, and

my recovery from it wasn't as straightforward as that, but these were certainly turning points in a process that led me to the person I am today. Some people might argue that as a professional sportsman, I am still monitoring what I eat. I suppose that's true, but the crucial difference for me is that I'm doing it to make myself stronger, channelling it in the right way. Recently, I came across a diary I'd written for the *Irish Times* during the 2020 Covid lockdown, and it made for an interesting read. 'I was so set on being the biggest on the pitch that I ate anything that came around. I remember during the Junior World Cup in Manchester, we went out to one of those all-you-can-eat steak places. They had to roll me home.' I remember that with joy. It was such a brilliant tournament and because all my family and friends could come over to see me play, it made it extra special. We had played the previous tournament in Italy and even though it was a great learning experience, Manchester was more fun – and we achieved our best result ever as runners-up. We beat New Zealand in the pool stages, and played Wales, Georgia and Argentina. There were so many players there who still play with me today and I'm proud of the fact that even though I was 130 kg at this point, I still managed to play close to eighty minutes.

Another really special win for me was my first European

Champions Cup in Bilbao with Leinster in 2018, against Racing 92. I studied Spanish in University College Dublin (UCD) and like to think I can hold a conversation, so Bilbao suited me just fine, but I have to admit I was disappointed with the weather. I had to pinch myself to realise that I was actually there as a bona fide member, ready to play for an incredible team. It was tight from the start, and the match was played in pouring rain, which made conditions really miserable. Racing were very physical right from the opening whistle, and every breakdown felt like a war, while Teddy Iribaren and Johnny Sexton traded penalties at each end.

I remember coming on at 66 minutes for Tadhg Furlong with the score at 9–6 to Racing. Every breakdown was a battle. In one carry I got chopped low and had to scramble to recycle. New Zealander Isa Nacewa, in his last game for Leinster, kicked a penalty to put us ahead 15–12 with two minutes to go. Then Racing pushed into our half and set up for a drop goal. I was on the edge of the ruck, heart pounding. When French international Rémi Talès struck it, I held my breath. It drifted wide. We'd done it! My first European title. I hugged Jack McGrath and we just laughed. We were soaked in sweat and rain but it didn't matter. That night we celebrated hard. I remember sitting on the hotel steps with a beer, just soaking it in. That win meant everything. It proved we could go toe to toe with the best in Europe and come out on top.

None of this would have been possible without the encouragement of Mr Jones and my dad. The rest was down to me. Having once been fixated on not eating, I was now focusing on getting as many nutrients as I could into my diet, tracking my intake on an app. I was eating four meals a day, which I poetically named 'meals one, two, three and four', basically consisting of protein in the form of chicken or meat, lots of vegetables and the right amount of carbohydrates – like rice or pasta – for energy.

My plates don't look all that pretty even today. I have three meals on rotation: ground beef, steak or eggs, with vegetables, rice and seasoning. If I'm going out, I like steak and spuds. I'm a true Irishman in that respect. Elaine gets sick of my cooking but hers is fantastic and unless I'm trying to drop a bit of weight, I'll eat anything she puts in front of me. I do find it hard in camp, though, where all the food is prepared for us: even though it's nutritious and balanced, I struggle to eyeball it and I'm much more comfortable preparing my own.

Nutritionists would say that athletes require between 1.6 g and 2.2 g of protein to build muscle, so I generally aim for 2.2 g of protein per kg of weight, so about 260 g, and my total calorie intake varies from 4,000 to 4,500 calories a day. Protein is really important because if we don't eat enough protein we risk more injuries. We do take nutritional supplements, but in the minimum quantities to help fuel recovery. Carbs are essential, particularly the slow-release ones that come from whole grains, fruit and veg, but simple carbs can be taken after a session to restore energy.

Nowadays, my weight has settled at around 118 kg. Because of my body weight and my job, I eat almost twice the average man's calorie intake, but then I'm burning it off. Endurance athletes would need to eat a lot more to fuel longer sessions of training; the swimmer Michael Phelps famously ate between 7,000 and 8,000 calories per day to fuel his long swims in the pool. I also try not to eat too much after my evening meal, keeping my meals and snacks within a window of time to maintain my usual weight. Overall, I stick to the 80–20 rule when it comes to eating – eating my regular diet 80 per cent of the time and treats roughly 20 per cent of the time – so that I can eat things I enjoy and not worry too much about it. I'm a fan of a burger and a glass of red wine if I'm treating myself. Other than that, I'm really a meat-and-potatoes man – a typical country boy!

The most important thing to a rugby player is hydration, because we can lose 3–4 kg during a match simply by sweating. The rule is generally to drink about a litre per kilogram to replenish the body – that's a lot of water. The coaching staff are very good at monitoring this and encouraging everyone to hydrate properly, particularly the younger lads, who might need a bit of encouragement in that department.

Looking back, I can see the evolution of the unhappy boy trying to control a very confusing world by not eating to the young man trying to maximise his strength and speed to the man I am today: someone who can look at myself in the mirror and think, *You're okay*. I'm finally comfortable in my own skin.

CHAPTER 4

FATHER AND SON

'Waste no more time arguing about what a good man
should be. Be one.'

Marcus Aurelius, Meditations

Dad is my biggest role model. Whether I'm playing for Leinster or Ireland, whether the crowd is big or small, when I come out on the pitch I can always find him in the crowd, no matter how big. While the national anthem is in full swing, I'll scan the stands for one of his two jackets, the blue one or the white one, and within seconds, there he'll be. Alone or with Mum's brother, Dave, Ernie will be there, and we'll make eye contact among the sea of faces. We joke that it's telepathy but I think it's because to me, he's both Mum and Dad at the same time.

I know that my mum Wendy would have given anything to be able to watch me play for my club and country but she never got the chance, so Dad is standing in for both of them, as he has since Mum died. I know that Mum is looking down on me as I play, urging me on, but how I wish she was here for the triumphs and the failures. In fact, I wish she was here to see all the good things in life: the birthdays and the Christmases, her children happy and settled, her in-laws, her grandchild … I would have loved her to see me get married to Elaine and to meet our son. But Dad's there and, I realise now, he always has been.

I know that, without Dad, I wouldn't be lining out with my teammates in some of the biggest stadiums in the world. I can't imagine where I'd be, to be honest. Sometimes, in the darkest days, I wondered if I'd even survive. The person who has been there through it all is Dad. Sometimes we fought, or we misunderstood each other, but he's always been there for me and I know that we share a lot of values: loyalty, hard work, resilience, caring. I know that he's proud of me and enjoys my success as a player: it's given him a great kick and he loves following me around the world. He has a great network now of the other players' parents: they even have their own WhatsApp group! They have a great time when we're on tour, arranging outings and dinners. I'm a bit envious … But I also know that he'd be proud of me and my two sisters no matter what we did.

For Dad and me rugby is very much a shared language. I can still remember trips with Dad down to Wesley to watch matches, sneaking onto the edge of the pitch to steal a ball or two and otherwise getting in the way. I can also remember my first medal; it was for a rugby blitz in Old Wesley. It was bronze with a gold velvet crest on it and I was unbelievably happy about that. Like so many little boys, I dreamt of being a rugby player when I grew up: I would examine the player profiles in the match programmes, look at their statistics and their backgrounds and think, *Could that be me?* I feel incredibly lucky that my dream came true.

When I was six or seven, though, all I thought was *this makes me happy.* Sport, unlike school, was where I could really excel. Even in my darkest days, sport was there for me. I also wanted to make Dad proud of me, almost to make up for what was going on by excelling on the rugby pitch. As a teenager, I wanted to compensate for that feeling that I was letting everyone down. I never set out to hurt my dad but it was a slippery slope that I wasn't able to stop myself going down – going out on the rugby pitch and doing well was my way of making things okay. Maybe I could make Dad happy by doing something that I liked but that he liked, too. To be good at the same thing meant so much to me.

We also shared a work ethic. Summers were all about Dad's family home in Clonegal, on the border between County Wicklow and County Carlow. It's a beautiful place, full of rolling hills and dark green forests. I'd spend hours in the fields herding sheep, helping with bringing in the hay and, in springtime, with lambing, which I loved. We'd have a duty rota for the lambing shed and because I'm an early riser, I would go out and sit there among the sheep, hearing their soft bleats and them shuffling around in the hay. I'd keep a close eye out for any sign that lambs were about to arrive and I became quite an expert midwife. I knew all the tricks: swinging the newborns around to get their hearts beating, clearing the mucus from their little nostrils so they could breathe, making sure that Mum was bonding with the newborn. Lambs are unbelievably cute but also unbelievably smelly. My sisters often tell me that me and my cousins used to practise our rugby skills on the adult sheep, tackling them when we were bringing them in for the night. No sheep were harmed, obviously.

It wasn't all about fluffy lambs, though: the job I hated most was picking stones out of the soil after the tractor had turned it over. As the youngest, I was given this job and it was back-breaking work, my cousin Rob supervising me from the tractor, telling me, 'You missed a bit there.' It certainly was an education in loving what you do, no matter what it is. Whenever I grumble about practice or training, I remember that I could be hunched over in a field in Carlow, picking stones and throwing them into a bucket.

I still loved the place, though. Dad is one of ten children, so there were a lot of cousins to hang out with. His eldest brother, Jimmy, inherited the farm when Granddad died, and when Jimmy passed away my cousin Rob took it over, along with my uncle George, who is my godfather. There was a twenty-year gap between Dad, who was the youngest in his family, and his eldest brother. Funnily enough, Mum was also the youngest in her family of five, along with Dave, who was my rugby coach in Wesley, Norman, my godfather, Brian and Hilary.

We loved going to the farm every summer as a family. In fact, we'd go down to Clonegal more or less every weekend, squeezing into the farmhouse along with any of Dad's brothers and sisters who might be visiting. One summer, we had to bring our own caravan because there were so many of us. Summers in Clonegal were about work, of course, but also about having fun outdoors, kicking a ball around. I had an improvised running track – down the driveway, along the narrow country lanes, back up through the fields then up a hill back to the house. I loved pulling tyres and testing my strength on random pieces of farm machinery. Horses were another passion and both Mum and Dad passed their love of horse riding down to us. There are so many photos of us on ponies down at the farm. My other favourite activity – when I got old enough – was driving the tractor. It was a small tractor, but I loved sitting up on the seat in the cab, driving away. I also learned to drive the digger and had some improvised driving lessons in the car from Dad. He'd stop the car at the bottom of the driveway and I'd sit on his knee and grip the steering wheel while he operated the pedals. We'd slowly make our way up the driveway to the house. I can't remember what age I was, but I must have been really young if I was able to sit on his knee.

Granny Violet was a proper, old-style granny. Dad's dad had died when he was eighteen, leaving Jimmy in charge of the farm, but Granny Violet ran the farmhouse, baking and cooking almost constantly, the kettle placed on the edge of the cooker in readiness for another cup of tea. One of her morning routines was to bring the ash bucket from the Aga down the driveway, pouring cold ashes into the potholes to fill them. An early example of recycling! She wasn't afraid to discipline me either: as a mum of ten, she knew exactly what to do. I loved and feared Granny Violet.

The work ethic I've inherited from Dad has really helped me to develop as a rugby player. Ability is only part of the equation: the rest is all about training and preparation. Ability has a ceiling, but hard work and effort doesn't. You can always do more, focus more on a certain area of your game, and when you know you've put in the work and really focused on putting right any errors, you're prepared for the big occasions. You're not relying on your talent but on the work you've put in. By the time you step out on the field, all that is done. You're ready. You'd be surprised what slogging away on a farm can teach you! But I also learned this from Dad: he never gave anything less than a hundred per cent, whether he was playing a round of golf, doing the garden or working.

As I grew older and Mum became more unwell, I would be sent down to the farm more regularly – I assume to spare me from some of the worst of her illness. There, Granny would take me under her wing and feed me from her stash of emergency cake and give me all the hugs I wanted. I'm sure she knew what we were all going through. Those days were all the more special because, even though I don't have a conscious sense of escaping what was going on at home, I must have felt it all the same.

When Mum died, Dad continued to work; he had to, with three of us in school. And being a man of that generation, who'd been to boarding school and who came from hard-working country people, he got on with it. I doubt that he shared his feelings about losing Mum with any of his friends. It just wasn't done. And so when I began to struggle I don't think he really knew how to deal with it.

Admittedly, I didn't give him much of a chance. I was fourteen, in my second year of secondary school, when things got really bad. I was shutting myself off completely from other people, telling myself, *Why is this their business? Just let me do my own thing.* You couldn't tell me anything. I was acting out, disappearing for days on end without telling him where I was going or what I was doing. I had a mobile phone but it was switched off when I didn't want any callers. I was drinking – and not with my friends in the park either. I was drinking alone, raiding the cocktail cabinet for vodka, filling a Ballygowan bottle and sneaking it out to drink, my thoughts spiralling as I did so.

Looking back, I can see that my dad was scared. He could see what I couldn't: a boy who was rapidly going off the rails, with him powerless to prevent it. I can imagine that he must have been terrified, but his straight-talking country ways were no match for the situation. And yet, he knew what was going on and he obviously cared because he arranged for me to see a therapist. He would bring me there every week, because he knew that if he didn't, I probably wouldn't have gone. It's only fifteen or sixteen years ago but back then, therapy wasn't as commonplace as it is now: I can see how far-sighted Dad was.

I can't really remember what myself and the therapist talked about in those sessions. It took a few sessions to break down the barriers – it was more just conversation, trying to find some commonality with a fourteen-year-old, which isn't easy. I think it was his idea to persuade Dad to get a dog for us, though. That's when Cheika the beagle came into our lives. The deal was that we would pick the dog and Dad would name him, which is why he's called after Michael Cheika, the inspirational former Leinster coach. He was a complete live wire and, like all beagles, had a mind of his own. There was no way we could let him off the lead because we'd have to chase him for five kilometres before we'd catch him. Cheika the dog became a very important part of our lives. In fact, Cheika passed away on the same weekend that we won the Six Nations in 2024. We had just returned to the hotel after the Scotland match when my sisters called me from the vet, checking to see if I was okay to say goodbye to Cheika over Facetime. I was incredibly grateful to them for giving me that opportunity. I felt a real mixture of joy and sadness then. Cheika had been there for all of us when things were really bad and even though he was old, it was still incredibly hard to say goodbye to him.

After my sessions, Dad would come to pick me up. This was the worst part: he'd hand over the cheque at the end of each session and I'd feel like shit. I felt such a deep sense of shame that my dad was paying for me and my problems. Was I worth it? Life was hard enough for Dad without having to fork out the cash for me.

My thought process was all over the place back then. I was in a vicious cycle of going to get help then hating myself for it. I would accept the lunches that Dad made for me then put them into the bin in school. I don't know if he knew, but my sisters and I spoke about it much later. I never realised what they were going through. I thought everyone was living their lives and that it was only me who was suffering like this. I can see now that that's not true, that my sisters were teenage girls trying to adjust to the loss of the woman in their lives, but back then I thought I was the only person in the world who felt like this. It's often said that death brings a family closer together. That's the Hollywood-movie version of it anyway. In our case, it didn't happen like that, or at least not for a long time. Life without Mum meant that we all disappeared into our rooms and Dad disappeared to work. We were all struggling but we were all doing it alone. Now, we're really close, but all those years ago, none of us could cope with it.

Back then, it wasn't long before I began to feel that it would be a lot easier for everyone if I wasn't here. The thoughts were fleeting at first but then became more concentrated. My mind went to dark places: how I'd do it and where. I spent the summer between first and second year in school on the farm, and one evening I went into one of the sheds. I scanned the place for the rope I'd seen a few days before. When I found it, I grabbed it and held it in my hand. I looked at it for what seemed like hours, thinking about flipping it over one of the rafters and forming a loop at one end. I could see it happen in slow motion, the rough feeling of the rope in my hand, the lightness as I swung it upwards … Then I heard a voice in my head: *Get the hell out of here.* I tossed the rope into the corner and ran out, shutting the door behind me. I went back inside the house as if nothing had happened.

I'm not sure why I didn't go ahead with it. I had attempted to overdose on paracetamol before, not taking enough to cause anything other than a headache. It's clear that thoughts of suicide reached a peak back then and then something happened to change that. I can't really say what it was, but perhaps it was my subconscious telling me that I had so much to live for. Maybe the thoughts of what it would do to Dad and my sisters saved me. Either way, I didn't go through with it and even though it would take me another couple of years to emerge from this period in my life, I never felt that low again.

The shed remains a closed door in my life. I never told anyone about it, because when I got over it, I felt, *It's gone. That person isn't me any more.* I thought, *I don't need to tell anyone this, because I'm a completely different person.* I worried that people would think that I didn't trust them enough to tell them the truth.

I do know that when I went back to school at the end of that summer of 2009, people found it hard to recognise me because I'd lost so much weight. Dad watched me carefully at this point and I knew that he was watching me. He'd want to see me eat so I'd eat, then go to the bathroom and throw up. One evening, when I came out of the bathroom, he was standing there, livid. We had a huge argument about it. I know now that he could see me disappearing before his eyes and he could do nothing to help me. His happy-go-lucky kid who loved his food had become the exact opposite. I couldn't see this. A few years ago, I found a few pictures of myself, one taken at twelve and the other at fourteen – I was looking at two different people.

The one thing that kept the lines of communication open between Dad and me was rugby. We both loved it, so that was the talking point, the motivation. When I wasn't eating, he'd reference the fact that I'd need to eat to play rugby. The fact that I wasn't doing well at school at that point was helped by the fact that I excelled at sport. Dad and I found a way of being together when he'd bring me to games and that neutral ground was so important to us. There was no need to talk about messy things like emotions or feelings. I like to think that rugby was the thing that kept us together at this point and I'm grateful for that.

I've spoken to my sisters about our teenage years a lot, but Dad and I haven't really talked. It's too painful. The closest we got was when we went out for a few pints a few months ago and we talked about everything: his childhood, which I didn't know a lot about, his time in boarding school, his playing days, his plans for the retirement he keeps telling us he's going to take – there's no sign of it yet! We did speak about what the years were like after Mum died. Dad was very level about it. His attitude was pragmatic, 'What could I do? I didn't have the time to feel sorry for myself when I had three children who depended on me.' Maybe that's true but I can't imagine what it would be like to try to get on with my life without Elaine in it. He had such a lot of inner strength.

I would like to ask him about me and him back then but I don't want to bring it up because I worry that bringing it up would be bringing it back for him. There would be too much to unpack with him, too much for him to take on. I think that speaking about it would put a burden on Dad and I don't want him to think that anything he did or didn't do was a factor in what happened in my life. I suppose I was shielding him from the sense that he wasn't enough, that he wasn't there for me, even though I understand exactly why. Perhaps I don't give him enough credit.

Dad has a great group of friends and they go to the pub together and play golf, but I don't think they talk about their feelings. I'm able to be a great deal more open than my dad was at the same stage in life. I can talk about my difficulties and my mental health publicly and people respond really well to that. It's clear that a lot of men out there are struggling, and sharing my story resonates with them. My dad didn't really have that chance and I often wonder how that affected him.

If I hadn't gone through what I did go through in those years, would I be the person I am today? Would Dad be the same person if he hadn't lost Mum? That's impossible to answer, but the Stoic philosophers call it *amor fati*, or a love of fate. To take the hand that fate deals you and play it as your own, or, as Nietzsche put it, 'Not merely [to] bear what is necessary, still less conceal it … but love it.'

Understanding this process, and learning to accept it, was the key to my recovery. I wasn't consciously aware of it, but reaching my own personal rock bottom, being faced with the stark reality of how low I'd gone, helped me to gradually work my way upwards. But it could so easily have gone the other way. When faced with a choice, I chose to live, but it's really such a split-second decision. All you can think is that you want to be out of pain, but what's a moment's thought for a distressed teenager is a lifetime of loss for a family. I can see that now.

Nowadays, a lot more is understood about teen mental health, and about the dangers of suicidal ideation. According to Youth Suicide Prevention Ireland, 'Ireland's suicide rate amongst adolescents aged 15–19 was 10.3 per 1,000 of population and ranks well above the national country average of 6.1 per 100,000' (https://yspi.ie). That's a frightening statistic. I'm not sure if it has to do with social media, but I can say that if social media had been around when I was a teenager, I'd have found it incredibly difficult to deal with. Having said that, much of the help that's now available comes on social media, such as text-based services for those experiencing thoughts of suicide. The pandemic was also a really tough time for young people – they lost out on so much, from school to socialising. In 2020, I was 24 and I could continue training at home, so I had something else to focus on. If I hadn't, I think my mental health would have suffered.

Back in 2009, not a lot was known about youth mental health. Nowadays, organisations like Pieta House do fantastic work, as do teenager-focused mental health organisations like Spunout. I am also proud to have contributed to Tackle Your Feelings, a programme for school students about mental wellbeing. Watching the animation of me, Elaine and our new dog, Pablo, for the programme always makes me smile.

In a weird way, now I can appreciate what I went through and why I went through it – to come out the other side. Being able to work through this period in my life is something I have accomplished and this knowledge has been a driving force ever since. I can say, *This is what I've been through. This is who I am.* And Dad, just by getting on with things, by protecting and providing for those he loved, has achieved the same thing. Our relationship proves that there is no 'right' way to grieve, but grief is something we both share, even if we deal with it in different ways. I also know that without Dad (and the other mentors who stepped into my life at critical times), I might not have made it. I owe him so much.

What would I say to teenage me now that those tough years are over? I would say that there is always something to live for, no matter how small. That the sense of isolation I felt back then wouldn't last for ever. That in a few years' time, I would look back and wonder if this unhappy person was the same me who now has a job I love, a family who supports me and a son of my own. None of this would have happened if I'd acted on a moment's impulse. There is always a bigger picture, a brighter future ahead of you, no matter how dark things are right now. The important thing is to keep on going. As Muhammad Ali said, 'Every day is different, and some days are better than others, but no matter how challenging the day, I get up and live it.'

CHAPTER 5

WHY CAN'T I JUST BE NORMAL?

'You're better off not giving the small things more time than they deserve.'

Marcus Aurelius, Meditations

Back in 2008, I had no idea that I was struggling with something other than just my grief at losing Mum, and it took me until 2023 to do something about it. I always knew that there was something not fully clicking into place, but I wasn't sure exactly what it was.

Let me talk you through a typical morning for me. I normally like to get up early because that's when I'm at my most productive. I love the peace and quiet of a 5 a.m. start and as a lifelong insomniac, it's a relief to be able to get the day started. I always begin with the best of intentions, with a clear idea in my head of what I want to do, but things often go astray and the day runs away from me. At the end of it, I can be exhausted, with a whole lot of unfinished tasks to show for my work and a sense of frustration about it.

One morning in May this year, I sat down to write an email about the gym that I was setting up – Three State in Dun Laoghaire – with my good friend from school, Josh Percival but left it half-written when I remembered that I needed to measure a window in the garage to be fixed. Off I went into the garage to measure the window, but then I spotted that a corner of the roof in the garage needed repairing, so I messaged a company on Instagram about that, at 7.30 a.m., before I remembered that the reason part of the roof was weak was because a stray tree branch was sticking into it, so it was time to get the chainsaw out. I was climbing a tree at seven-thirty in the morning with a chainsaw to cut down a tree branch! That done, I came back inside the house, opened my phone and remembered the half-written email. I finished it, before remembering that a delivery had arrived the previous day. Off I went to the front porch, carried in the box containing my brand-new strimmer, then I noticed that one of the fuel tanks for the strimmer was only half-full, so I called the company to let them know. By this stage, it was still only eight o'clock in the morning. This is life inside my brain!

I know – I could have finished the email and *then* remembered the window in the garage, but if I don't do something immediately, I'll forget all about it. Sometimes it can feel as if I'm not in control of my thought process,

Getting started early!

With my mum, Wendy

The Porter Family

With Mum, Erica and Leigh at the Cliffs of Moher

Meeting the GOAT, Jonah Lomu, with my cousin David

With Leo Cullen, a fellow mascot and Des Dillon when I was a mascot for Leinster

In action at mini rugby

Winning at Old Wesley

U10s at Old Wesley – I'm holding the ball

My early teens, with Erica and Leigh, and Cheika the dog

Playing schools rugby with St. Andrew's with James Ryan in pursuit for St. Michael's

Hitting the dirt at St. Andrew's

Above: Winning the colours with Erica and Leigh

Left: 2015 – winning the Leinster League with UCD in Donnybrook

At an Ireland U20s game with Dad, Erica and Leigh

Getting my first Irish U18s schools cap with my dad, Ernie

with thoughts pinging all over the place, like the metal ball in a pinball machine. I can be doing lots of jobs, firing on all cylinders, but either they aren't the ones I set out to do that day, or they get half-done before I remember the next thing. It's called life with ADHD.

I think that's why I love the structure of my life as a professional rugby player: there are no random balls shooting at me – at least, only oval-shaped ones – there are no rabbit-holes of social media down which I can disappear for hours, there are no items or events to forget. I know what I'm doing and when and where I'm doing it. It's a huge relief because I know that if I didn't have that framework, life could feel pretty chaotic.

I'm happiest when I'm out in the garden, pulling weeds and digging, and I can pass hours happily enjoying the process. I find that the repetitive work outdoors helps to calm my thoughts, which are constantly in motion. I now know why but as a child, I had no clue that my hyperactivity might have had a neurological cause. I was simply someone who 'needed to be run', as a relative put it, like an energetic collie! It's true that I rarely slept as a child and one of my earliest memories is of sitting on my parents' bedroom floor in the middle of the night, playing with Lego Duplo, so I must have been really young. To this day, I can survive on a few hours' sleep a night: handy when you're a new parent and your partner needs a rest. That's one of the best things about my new job of being a dad – just me and my little boy in the middle of the night. It feels as if we are the only two people awake in the whole world.

I know, however, that I'm one of the lucky ones when it comes to living with ADHD. My brain is ideally suited to the single-mindedness that's needed in professional sport. I can really use that hyperfocus to zone in on what I'm doing and keep pushing. The same applies to the gym: because I love it, I'll happily spend time on it. In fact, when I first started working out, in Ben Dunne's gym in Sandyford, I became hooked to the extent that at one point, I seriously considered giving up rugby because I was so into the gym! The very same issues that can be destructive for some are helpful to me.

When I was a kid, though, it wasn't as straightforward. Both Mum and Dad got me involved in sport to get rid of some of my excess energy. Tennis, hurling, soccer, rugby – you name it, I tried it. Rugby was what stuck. As soon as I took the ball in my hand, I thought, *This is for me. This is something I can be good at.* It came as a huge relief to me because school was something I wasn't good at. I found it hard to sit still and pay attention and my school reports were, let's say, interesting. The teacher's comments at the bottom of the reports were a series of negatives: doesn't pay attention; doesn't like to stay quiet, doesn't participate, constantly interrupting – that kind of thing. It wasn't a lack of effort: I knew that I couldn't do well, no matter how hard I tried. Something wasn't clicking into place. I used to find homework a nightmare. I can still remember poor Dad coming home from work and having to sit for hours with me, but somehow the information wouldn't go in. It wasn't that I didn't understand the concepts, it was that I couldn't seem to get them to go into my brain and reproduce them on the page. Or if I did remember them for a test, they'd disappear once the test was done.

As a result, in primary school I was a bit of a messer and I can still remember spending a lot of time in a room by myself. I must have been sent there so that I wouldn't disrupt the class. It wasn't much fun. When the teachers were really desperate, they'd send me in to one of my sister's classrooms to sit with them and behave. The teachers may have thought that this benefited me, but it didn't really. I wasn't doing it on purpose, and I wasn't getting anything out of being excluded.

But it never even occurred to me that I might have ADHD. I had actually been tested for it in primary school – the results were inconclusive – but Mum and Dad had a folder of my school reports and all the signs seemed to point to it. Still, even though nowadays diagnosis is almost routine, even twenty years ago not a lot was known about it. I persisted in trying to fit myself into the academic mould, though, and worked really hard for my Leaving Cert. For the first few years in St Andrew's, I hadn't wanted to be there, but in fifth year I made the decision to get my head down and study. It felt important to me to work hard to prove to myself that I could and that I could even do reasonably well. I persuaded Dad to pay for study club after school and I got my head down and studied hard. If you have ADHD, there's nothing better than a deadline – it really focuses the mind.

Even so, I found distraction really hard to deal with and subjects like maths were difficult, because it needed to be taught and I struggled to concentrate for long enough to take the concepts in. I can remember willing myself to focus, but my attention always seemed to wander and I'd come around from my daydream completely lost. I was quite good at chemistry, biology and geography, because I loved the factual nature of those subjects, and I really liked my chemistry teacher, Mr Hehir – he was from the no-bullshit school of teaching and I found his teaching style helped me to focus. I found English really tough, though, as it's far from factual, but I was surprisingly good at Spanish. It's a bit rusty now, but I can still just about hold a conversation. In the end, I did pretty well in my Leaving Cert. I was quite pleased, given that I'd also fitted in training, meal-prep and rugby around my studies. It had taken an enormous amount of effort, and I didn't yet know why that was, but I got there in the end.

I went to UCD to study Spanish, geography and economics, but it took me seven years to do my degree. Looking back, I got caught in that trap of thinking *everyone's going to college, so I'd better go too*, but I would have been better suited to training for a practical job – anything outdoors. I'm not suggesting that people should ditch the degree in favour of their dreams – at the time I was in the Leinster Academy, but there was no guarantee that I'd make it in professional sport – it was just that the academic path wasn't right for me.

I'd love to say that my UCD days were the best of my life, but really, rugby took first place. It had to, even though there were no guarantees that I'd make it in the professional game. Rugby was my passion and I wanted to give it everything to see if I could progress. By this stage, I was training four times a week with the Leinster Sub Academy and playing matches for UCD on a Saturday, so it was full on. I had a sports scholarship and the university was very accommodating, letting me take two modules instead of six in a semester and giving me support to keep me on track, but I didn't have the full college experience. There were no Dicey's Mondays student nights with cheap drinks for me! No three-quid pints in the college bar or L&H (Literary and Historical Society) debates. I missed out on that side of things, but I made up for it by keeping in touch with my schoolfriends, whom I still see today, and by having some great nights out with the UCD rugby team. When I graduated in 2021 I didn't feel that I'd missed out, because I'd achieved my dream of playing professionally, but sometimes I wish I'd had a bit more fun.

The turning point for me and ADHD was moving in with Elaine. My family were used to my ways, but she found herself living with someone who could start seven things at once and finish one of them; who would leave things in random places; and who, unless he had a list in front of him, couldn't prioritise for the life of him. I can still remember our wedding preparations: Elaine had a ring binder with details of everything in it, separated into different files. I had a Post-it note with a few things scribbled on it, which I eventually lost. It wasn't that I didn't care – it was that this was the way I did things. I never realised that there was anything wrong with it until I was living with someone else. The thing is, I would often find it really frustrating. Why was I the way that I was? Why did I hold up an entire flight to Barcelona on our first holiday together because I'd left my phone in the departure lounge? That incident still embarrasses me: the doors were about to close for take-off when I realised that I'd left my phone behind.

Maybe, as Elaine gently pointed out to me, I could make my life easier by getting an assessment to confirm whether I had ADHD. Elaine is right about most things, so I went off to get an assessment. I had to do a whole range of cognitive tests and provide lots of school reports and feedback from my family and others who knew me well. The results were really interesting. I found that while I was in the 95th percentile when it came to problem-solving, where I fell down was when it came to attentiveness. That and prioritising and processing information. And my insomnia was a giveaway, I learned.

'You'd be surprised how many professional athletes actually have ADHD,' the psychologist told me. 'Sport is something they can focus on and because they enjoy it, it works to their advantage.'

A lightbulb went off in my head. Maybe that's why, when I was fifteen and I decided that in order to play rugby to a high level, I'd need to eat, and I'd need to get bigger, I focused on that to the exclusion of everything else. I'd studied videos of body-builders, developing an obsession with Arnold Schwarzenegger in particular.

At the time, he was huge, both physically and in films like *Conan the Barbarian* and *Terminator*, a real icon who made bodybuilding into a global phenomenon. Like my hero, I went to the gym relentlessly, even missing my sister Leigh's graduation from secondary school and dinner afterwards because I didn't want to skip a session. She still slags me about it, but I wish I'd gone.

I was so focused on the gym that Dad began to worry about me. Once, he said, 'You're spending all this time in the gym, but what else have you got planned for your life?' I didn't really listen. I had a project now and that project was me. I didn't know if I had what it took to be a professional, but there was only one way to find out, I thought. I could see how dedicated Arnie and others like him were, not just to bodybuilding but to improving themselves. In the same way, I felt that I wasn't just building up my body in a physical sense, I was building a wall around myself. When I was younger, I would have been picked on for being fat. Now, no one would pick on me any more. My size would be a suit of armour for me.

At first, I used to train just for the love of it. Mr Jones had taught me the basics of getting the form right and lifting safely, so off I'd go every morning to Ben Dunne's gym, arriving there at 6 a.m. and staying until it was time to leave for school. I would be in the gym for up to three hours, trying to emulate Arnie and other big-name bodybuilders, their style of training and the dedication and structure around the routines. I knew that I had to put in a lot of time to get the rewards. I focused on powerlifting, which includes bench presses, deadlifts and squats. I can remember the deadlift in particular, as the bar would rub off my shins over and over again, until the blood was dripping on my feet. At my biggest, when I was going hammer and tongs at the gym and maxing out, I could squat 325 kg, deadlift 300 kg for about three reps and bench press a measly 190 kg. A lot of my coaches have told me that you can't be good at all three lifts, which comes as a relief, because I have got a lot of slagging for my bench presses. Now, my shoulder joint is like a coat hanger, so I'm not as good as I used to be. However, it must run in the family, because my sister Leigh has competed as a powerlifter nationally.

After the gym came school. I'd sit on the bus into St Andrew's, snap my Beats headphones on, heavy metal blasting in my ears, and I would write down ideas for new gym routines, to test myself and to try out after rugby training with Mr Jones. As my playlist – Slipknot, Anthrax, Amon Amarth, Metallica and Iron Maiden – rang in my ears, I'd write down ideas. In school, Mr Jones taught us a lot about fitness and conditioning, getting us to do sled pushes, tyre lifts, hill sprints. I can remember doing fitness training in the snow a few times. The training gym in St Andrew's at the time consisted of a shipping container that Mr Jones had kitted out with equipment, and I loved the no-frills vibe. I was determined to keep pushing until I was the biggest in my class and in my year. Being uncomfortable and doing really tough sessions was an outlet for me as well as a distraction from everything else that was going on in my life. I also loved getting praise and validation from Mr Jones, whom I really admired. He obviously knew my situation when I came in as a thirteen-year-old and he knew the value that training had for anyone going through difficulties. I began to grow in confidence as I grew stronger. I was accountable to no one other than myself, and that made me feel good about myself. The onus was on me to get up early and to get to the gym before school. For the first time in a long time, I was happy.

With my new diet and gym routine, I put on twenty kilos between fifth and sixth year in St Andrew's. We had a great rugby team that year, with four of us on the Irish under-18s: myself, Greg Jones, Johnny Guy and Jordan Larmour. Greg Jones was our captain the whole way up through school, and if anyone was going to turn professional, it was him. He was one of the smartest players in the game: everyone said it. He was truly exceptional. At this point, I wasn't exceptional. But what I did have was that obsessional focus. At the beginning of sixth year, I was getting up at 5 a.m. to make my breakfast: six raw eggs mixed with oats and berries – a sort of raw cake batter! I'd swig this out of a big measuring jug and I'd usually have do two batches because it wouldn't all fit in the blender. Then I'd walk down to the Luas stop in Cherrywood, rain or shine, and head to the gym. Then I'd get the bus to school, just about making it in time for registration, after which I'd crack out a lunchbox full of chicken and rice for two – at nine in the morning. Chicken, rice, tuna, pasta – any concoction I could think of with the addition of a good few shakes of hot sauce, and down it would go to fuel training and then another session in the gym. When I went out with my friends, I'd tuck into two huge portions of whatever they were eating because I'd burn both off in the gym later. I dropped into the school a few years after I left and my old rugby coach Mr Jones fondly recalled me walking around the school with big boxes of Tupperware. I would also carry around a three-litre plastic carton of milk and would swig from it regularly. My father had to start buying fifty-pound trays of chicken breasts from the wholesalers to keep me in protein, to his huge relief. I'd gone from being one of the smallest guys in my year to one of the biggest, and it felt good to get that control back in my hands. I could have been a jock but was saved by my friends' slagging.

I'd also argue that my ADHD helped me to really zone in on improving myself: I suppose I wanted that feeling that what I was doing, and not what someone else was doing, was going to benefit me. I wanted to work hard and see results and with gym work, you can really see that. Your ultimate competitor is yourself. I could put that problem-solving part of me to good use doing something I truly enjoyed.

How I train now is quite different. For a start, I'm on a team, so I'm training for my position, but at the end of a long season, it's really the minimum effective dose to maintain form. I can't afford to max out in the gym because I'll need to play properly on a Saturday. We don't chase big weights and high reps but instead focus more on strength and power, with lower reps and moving weights fast. We'd have a bit more volume on a Monday but taper off towards the end of the week. We also focus a lot on rest and recovery days now. I'm a big fan of ice baths for muscle recovery, and saunas, massage, etc. But the best way of recovering is being able to fully switch off. Stress is a real problem as a player, because if your cortisol levels are high, it inhibits your ability to recover. There's nothing like going for a walk or being with family and friends. I also love being out in the garden, headphones on, listening to country music. I'm a big fan of the classic country stars like Johnny Cash, Willie Nelson and Conway Twitty, and they are the perfect soundtrack to my weeding and digging. My relatives in Carlow are huge fans of Garth Brooks and Zach Bryan and always come up to Dublin for concerts, kitted out in the cowboy hats.

When I first came in to the Leinster Sub Academy in Donnybrook in 2014, they had to rein me in a bit, because I'd often do two sessions – one there and one in the UCD gym. My coach, Dave Fagan, used to keep an eye out for me in UCD and warn me not to overdo it. He was known for being a really tough trainer, but I thought I knew everything there was to know about training. I had to learn to train with a different structure and to learn things specific to rugby, instead of just sweating away all the time, but I was a willing student and I think I passed the Dave Fagan test.

Dave's job was to see if we had what it took to get to the professional level. At this point, though, there was no guarantee at all that I'd get into the Academy itself. The Sub Academy is the first step for a lot of guys when they leave school. The idea is that in year one, you're in the Sub Academy, and in year two, you'd hopefully get into the Academy itself. It took me two years to get into the Academy because of my birth date, which is in January. While that might seem like a disaster, I feel it was a huge stroke of luck. At the time, I don't think I was as good or as experienced as some of my contemporaries, so that second year really benefited me. I wouldn't have made it straight off the bat in my first year: my rugby skills were too raw because I was still learning my game and I wasn't getting much game time, because I was playing for UCD under-20s as well, and I wasn't getting picked that much. I can't say that the coach liked me all that much. That can happen, but it can't be an obstacle unless you make it into one.

In my second year, I made a huge leap forward. I got stuck into the gym, ate all around me and had a great coach in Dave Fagan, who sadly passed away in 2024. He reminded me a bit of my school coach, David Jones, in that he was a bit of a maverick. Maybe I felt like a maverick, too, because of the way my mind worked and because of what I'd been through. Whatever the reason, we clicked. At Sub Academy level, they're looking to separate the wheat from the chaff, to see if you have what it takes to play professionally when you're not fully developed in your game. They want to see how hard you're willing to work to get your place, to wear that Leinster jersey. Even if you have all the talent in the world, you might not make the grade because you aren't putting in the work.

I think it was hard for guys who'd been really good at the game their whole lives: they expected to continue to be good, to be picked because of that. Often, they were really skilled in one area of the game and expected that to make up for any deficiencies, whereas others knew that hard work and diligence in training and a willingness to improve on weaknesses would see them through. That – and not going out on the lash when you have training the next morning!

It takes a single-mindedness to achieve that and I think that's what I had going for me. Other guys were more talented, but that focus was my super-power. That and a willingness to put everything into it – not to hold back. I've always felt that if you put a lot of time into something and you don't succeed, you might wonder what the point was, but when you really put time and effort into something, even if you don't reap the rewards, it's still a win. You'll never regret making the effort and coming up short. You might regret not trying, though.

It's an interesting conundrum to me as a player how much of the game is down to raw talent and how much is down to effort and persistence. It's such an elusive thing, ability: it can fade over time, or it can be harnessed with work to be much more than its original form. Some of the greatest talents have faded in the arena while others have gone on to do great things. Serena Willams was and is an amazing tennis player and athlete and yet she freely admits that sheer hard work was what really mattered. 'Luck has nothing to do with it, because I have spent many, many hours, countless hours, on the court working for my one moment in time, not knowing when it would come.' The great soccer player Pelé used to get up in the dark to practise his soccer skills. When asked why he played in the dark, he replied that it was because they had no electricity! You see what I mean.

Recently, I came across something David Beckham said in a conversation with Rio Ferdinand in his interview series *Rio Meets*. He was talking about the soccer giant Lionel Messi. What he said was really interesting. 'The first day he arrived at our training ground [Inter Miami] he arrived at 6.50 in the morning and there was no one around except for one guy to let him in ... and the team weren't training till ten.' To Rio Ferdinand's question, 'What's he doing then?' Beckham answered, 'Preparing. Preparing. He's in the gym, he's warming up, he's doing all of the things you expect a young kid to do. And he's still doing them at his age [thirty-seven].' What Beckham didn't add was that he, too, was famous for staying on the pitch long after everyone else had left, practising his shots.

I'm not comparing myself to these giants, obviously, but the point about needing to work hard and to prepare at any point in your career is one that resonates with me. You can have all the talent you want, but if you're not prepared to work hard and prove that you're a team player, you'll struggle. I often compare my career in rugby to rock climbing. When you're on the cliff face you look up to see if there's any ledge above you to grab onto. You see a tiny crevice in the rock and you reach up and grab hold of it and pull yourself up. Then you're there. You keep looking up for the next foot- or hand-hold, you grab hold of that and you keep climbing.

CHAPTER 6

KEEP CLIMBING

'Look well into thyself; there is a source of strength
which will always spring up if thou wilt always look.'

Marcus Aurelius, **Meditations**

In my own case, I knew that I had some kind of talent, but as a teenager, I went to a lot of trials and never got selected. From the day that John Fogarty told me that I wasn't big enough, I thought, *This isn't going to happen again. I'm not going to lose out again.* And the way I would do this was through training and preparation. There's a ceiling on ability, but there are no limits to the amount of preparation and training you can do. When you know you've put in the work and put your focus into something that will really benefit your game, you're halfway there.

Maybe that's easy for me to say now but, at the time, there were no guarantees. In fact, I can still remember the pep talk that Dad gave me on that very subject. He wanted me to be realistic, I know; to consider what might happen if I didn't become a professional. 'What's your Plan B?'

he asked me. I really had no idea. I had talent but it wasn't at all clear that I had what it took to make it to play for my province and my country. It would take a lot of hard work, some lucky breaks and a fortuitous change of position to get me to where I wanted to be. That and what some people might call obsession but I call laser focus. Maybe that's what made the difference for me – but who knows?

My ADHD brain can make things tricky sometimes, but on more than one occasion it's really helped me to push forward, to climb over obstacles with a single-mindedness that I've found really helpful. At the time, I didn't realise that my obsessive focus was due to neurodiversity: I just took it for granted that this was what it took to be a professional sportsperson. Sometimes, we don't see things as opportunities until they've passed us by, but thankfully, I was able to grab mine and to hang on for dear life.

I got my first cap for Leinster against the Italian side Treviso on 2 September 2016 at the opening of the Guinness Pro12 season. I was sub for Jack McGrath as a loosehead and I was scrumming at the same time as Mike Ross. It was my first year on the senior team and I was a raw 21-year-old.

I was named on the bench and spent the first half with my heart thumping, waiting for the call. I knew I'd done my homework; I just had to keep reminding myself of that. I was ready. Leinster had a strong team that day, including plenty who also played on the Irish team, such as Cian Healy, Josh van der Flier and Rob Kearney, to name just a few. It was incredible to think I'd be playing alongside them in a proper game. Treviso hadn't had a great few seasons, but they seemed to be determined to turn things around with their new head coach, former All Black Kieran Crowley. Taking a Leinster scalp at the RDS would be huge for them. We couldn't let that happen. I couldn't let the team down.

It was Jamison Gibson-Park's and Joey Carbery's first game too, and things couldn't have gone better for Joey. He scored a try within the first three minutes, and a second twenty minutes later. Treviso came back at us with a try of their own by Italy international Marco Fuser, but by the time I came on soon after half-time we had the measure of them. My first scrum was a blur. I hit low, drove hard and felt the pressure of professional rugby for the first time. Treviso were physical, but we controlled the tempo. I remember chasing a kick down the right wing, lungs burning, and getting stuck into a ruck near the touchline. It wasn't a flashy performance, but I did my job. Another try by James Tracy and a conversion and penalty by Fergus McFadden gave us a secure win, 20–8. I was thrilled, but even more hugely relieved. My first game and we'd won. I could see Ernie in the stands with a huge smile on his face. In the changing room, the older lads gave me a nod. That meant everything. I didn't sleep much that night. I kept replaying the scrums, the carries, the noise. I knew I had a long way to go, but I also knew I belonged. That was the start of it all.

Coming out on the pitch that day was nerve-racking. Now, I'm fine with the big occasions but back then I was so nervous that I'd get sick before every game. The anxiety would make my stomach churn and next thing, I'd throw up. Then a fellow player gave me a good piece of advice: use the crowd's energy like a battery, soak it up and use it to push myself forward. It worked and instead of being overawed by the situation, I managed to settle into the game.

The game also gave me my first glimpse of that elusive thing we call a flow state. Ever since it was brought into the public domain by psychologist Mihaly Csikszentmihalyi back in the 1970s, people have studied this state, when everything seems to come together and work becomes almost automatic, with time falling away and everything happening without the person even trying. As you can imagine, sports people are really interested in this idea and I've experienced it for myself. It doesn't happen from the get-go: I have to build into the game and really become involved, but everything gets going for me at around the fifty-minute mark. I often describe it as getting my second wind in a game, where everything clicks: I somehow get on the end of some good carries and some good tackles and I feel a burst of increasing self-confidence. I find that I'm able to slow down the moment I'm in and it feels like the ball isn't being whipped at me, but is coming at me almost in slow motion, when I get myself into a good tackle or get forward in a scrum, my legs weightless, all my anxiety gone. My mind isn't consciously thinking; it's just acting for my body. My teammate Caelan Doris is really interested in the flow state and the psychology around it. Apparently, those of us with ADHD can struggle to achieve it, but I can confirm that that's not the case. When it happens, it's magic.

It wasn't that long after the Treviso game that it was suggested I move from the position of loosehead to tighthead, from the number 1 jersey to number 3 at the other side of the scrum. I wasn't at all sure. Stuart Lancaster was the coach then and he said, 'Look, you've got the strength, the body size and shape and all that. What would you think about moving to the other side of the scrum?' I was comfortable where I was, even though there was a lot of competition for the loosehead spot in Leinster.

Cian Healy was going strong, as were Peter Dooley and Jack McGrath. Tadhg Furlong had pretty much claimed tighthead for himself and was doing brilliantly, as was Michael Bent. If anything, I'd be a third string there.

When anyone presents you with change, it's always a challenge. Even more so when it looks as if you'll have to take a step backwards to achieve it. Moving from loosehead to tighthead isn't just about moving from one side of the scrum to the other, of course. It's about body positioning to hold the weight of the scrum and putting the opposing tighthead under pressure with sheer downward force. As a loosehead my job would be to keep things nice and steady for my hooker while some giant of a tighthead was pushing me towards the ground. Now that I'm back at loosehead in the Irish set-up, I'm up against guys like Uini Atonio, the French tighthead who weighs in at a mere 149 kg to my 118 kg and six foot six to my six foot. It's like pushing against Mont Blanc. In our few encounters, I've definitely come off worse.

That's why our win against France in Marseille in the 2024 Six Nations meant so much. The Stade Vélodrome was packed and the French crowd were in full voice. We hadn't won there in years. We started fast. Jamison Gibson-Park and Calvin Nash got us going, then Joe McCarthy made a huge impact. I remember one scrum just before half-time where we drove them back five metres. That gave us a lift. France came back hard. Penaud scored and the place erupted. But we stayed calm. I carried off a lineout in their 22 and we built pressure. Jack Crowley kicked well, kept the scoreboard ticking. Then came the moment. Antoine Dupont, their scrum-half, went down after a collision and the momentum changed. We took control. I made a key tackle on Cameron Woki late on that helped force a turnover. The final score was 38–17, which I think made a statement. We'd gone to France and dominated.

That doesn't mean that I'm not a bit more apprehensive when I'm playing against the French or South African packs, just because of their sheer size and strength. They're renowned for having heavy front rows and are tough lads to beat. Both countries pride themselves on their huge packs and huge tightheads. I have a lot more confidence in myself now, and in the lads around me. I know that I'm capable of doing the job and so are they, so I tend not to get fazed by other front rows. When I first started out with Ireland and I was scrumming against England's tighthead prop Dan Cole, I'd find it tough going, because he was so experienced. He's about ten years older than me, so by the time I encountered him, he'd already been on two Lions tours and played in four World Cups, as well as winning three Six Nations tournaments. He retired in 2025 and I'd love to have as long a career as him.

Ellis Genge, the England loosehead, started out around the same time as me. I played him as a young tight-head and I did not have a great day in the scrums. I tend not to think about games too much after I play them, but I can remember a couple of times after playing Ellis thinking, *That was a hard day at the office*.

Before the Lions tour this year, my experience of Genge was coming up against him in matches, often the Six Nations. There'd be all kinds of shit talk going on and we'd be needling each other in games. Now, on the Lions tour of Australia, we're sharing a room and he's the nicest guy you'll ever meet. I tease him that he's a terrible roommate, with his awful snoring, but mine's pretty bad too – I've broken my nose too many times. I'm not always the tidiest of roommates. Not to mention that my pillows always look like something from the *Texas Chainsaw Massacre* with my constantly bleeding cauliflower ears after years of scrummaging.

Genge and I have developed a close bond. He's an incredible guy, an incredible player, and it's been great to build a friendship with him. He's also one of the best in the business so it's great being able to learn from each other along the way. We probably could have just as easily not liked each other, as we were competing for the same spot on the team. But I was slapping him on the back when he was named to start in the first test, and he was the first to congratulate me when I was named for the second. He even handed me my Lions jersey and cap during our ceremony. I still have one of his jerseys, too, from an old Ireland–England match. I've told him I'm going to hang it in my gym.

Back in 2016, however, the main issue for me wasn't actually practising the position. It felt as if I was going into reverse, stopping my progress as a player to return to my club, UCD, when I thought I was getting into the Leinster set-up. I mean no disrespect to UCD, but I thought my days there were over and I was on to bigger and better things! I thought long and hard about it before deciding to trust in the Leinster coaches. If they had a bigger plan, I'd do my best to fit into it.

I went back to UCD and to the new position of tighthead, playing in lots of games until I really had the hang of it. Even so, a voice in my head kept saying, *I've got my Leinster cap. Why am I taking a step back?* As any athlete will know, we are our own worst critics. The thing is, we can't see into the future, so this tighthead move felt like an experiment, albeit a reasonable one. I have to admit to being quite closed-minded about it at first, but then

I thought, *Don't be second-guessing either yourself or your coaches: just get on with it.* So I threw myself into the new role and vowed to make the best of it.

I wasn't sure if I was succeeding, but at the time Mike Ross spoke about the switch to *The 42*: 'He's looking pretty good, to be honest ... The kid is really strong, Cian Healy is kind of looking at him a bit enviously. I shouldn't have said that, he'll hear that and be angry with me ... it's quite tough to switch over to that side but he's improving every week. You can see it, he's figuring it out.' I didn't know about this at the time. All I could think was that the period of my apprenticeship seemed to last for ages, but actually it was more like a season, from September to June. By the end of that year, 2017, I got my first cap for Ireland as a tighthead. The experiment had worked and I was off to the United States with the Ireland team, then on to Japan.

The very first game was in New Jersey, maybe not the natural home of rugby, but I was so elated to be playing I didn't care. With eleven Irish players off to New Zealand on Lions duty during the summer of 2017, I got my opportunity to make my debut, alongside five others. The dressing room in the Red Bull Arena was pumping with Bruce Springsteen's 'Glory Days' as we got ourselves psyched up to play the USA Eagles on 10 June. Music always gets me going, but to hear The Boss roaring the classics in a New Jersey stadium was special. The other boss, Joe Schmidt, had ensured that the squad environment was competitive and we'd been driven hard in training, which was just as well as the 31-degree heat would be like an extra opponent, sapping your energy.

I watched the sea of green in the crowd roaring with joy as Keith Earls got our first try. He seemed to be everywhere on the pitch, setting up Jacob Stockdale for another try and then getting a third himself. Things were looking good, but I was anxious to get onto the pitch, to be part of it. By the time I came on in the second half the score was a comfortable 36–7, but the USA started to come at us strong. John Quill (who is from Cork!) got a try for the Eagles, and they were looking to get the upper hand in scrums. I was buzzing with nerves. My first scrum came just inside our 22. I locked in, felt the hit and held my ground. That settled me. I got a couple of carries, nothing spectacular, but I made sure I got over the gain line. I remember one tackle against Ryan Matyas near halfway that got a cheer from the Irish fans. That gave me a lift. Then my Leinster teammate James Ryan, a fellow international debutant, got a try with his first touch of the ball! Incredible stuff. I was straight over to pat him on the back. The Americans didn't really bother us after that, and the game remained in our control. We won 55–19 in the end, but for me it was about more than the score. It was about wearing the jersey, feeling the weight of it and knowing I'd earned it. There's a great photo of me and James Ryan, a fellow rookie, standing on the field after the match, both of us so proud.

The most important thing to me though was that Dad was there to see it. I can still remember clambering up onto the hoarding and looking down at the seven-foot drop, before shoving myself forward into the crowd and more or less crowdsurfing up to Dad and my uncle Dave. I gave them both a huge hug. It meant so much to me that Dad was there to see me get my very first Irish cap and I travelled on to Japan with a new-found sense of pride.

Until this point, I don't think I'd ever thought that I could make a career in professional rugby. In childhood, it had been a dream, which I lost for a while in secondary school, before picking it up again at the Leinster Sub Academy and then the Academy itself. The step back to UCD had been an opportunity, I now realised, not a demotion. And I credit my iron-clad focus for getting me there. I may struggle to organise my day, or to digest big chunks of information – and don't ever ask me for directions – but when I love something, I am capable of going for it with an almost scary determination.

The funny thing is that all through the match I was more worried about having to sing a song to mark my first cap than the game itself. All I could think was, *Oh, God I have to sing a song after.* Normally, they keep these rituals to the dressing room, but nope, I would be getting up in front of a packed function room, with all the players from both teams, plus their families, to belt out a song. Anyone who has heard me sing will know that I'm not naturally gifted in that department. I stumbled through Men at Work's 'Down Under', and quickly retreated.

Eight years after my big switch, I am back where I started. I'm a loosehead and happy to be one, but I'm also happy that I learned to shift up a gear and that change isn't as scary as you might think.

I'm also pleased that I can breathe again now! There's less pressure coming through you at loosehead. Also, as a tighthead, you're expected to scrum first and then let everything else fall into place. As a tighthead you're standing up trying to catch your breath after a while, sometimes trying not to pass out when you're seeing stars, but as a loosehead you're trying to attack more and lock it down. I'm happy where I am, but I'm glad I've done both. It's like being able to write with both my left and right hand. My exposure at tighthead definitely helps me now – I have a unique perspective on what a tighthead is trying to do to me.

I am also glad that I got my ADHD diagnosis because it helps me to understand myself better and to know what makes me tick. I have chosen not to take medication, because my exercise regime helps me so much, and my strict work schedule, but I know it's benefited many, many others. I say, do what works for you. And focus on the big stuff, like family and friends, not the things that matter less. And, while I'm happy to be open about my ADHD, it doesn't define me. It doesn't come first on my CV. I don't credit it with my success in sport, but neither do I think *I can't do this because I have ADHD*. I can and I have done it. It may not be the way everyone else would do it, but it's done.

CHAPTER 7

THIS IS MY CHANCE

Stuart Lancaster once sent me a quote by Theodore Roosevelt and I often take it out and read it when things are tough. You might know it as 'The Man in the Arena', and it goes like this:

> The credit belongs to the man who is actually in the arena, whose face is marred by dust and sweat and blood, who strives valiantly, who errs and comes up short again and again, because there is no effort without error or shortcoming, but who knows the great enthusiasms, the great devotions, who spends himself in a worthy cause; who, at the best, knows, in the end, the triumph of high achievement, and who, at the worst, if he fails, at least he fails while daring greatly, so that his place shall never be

with those cold and timid souls who knew neither victory nor defeat.

I often come back to this quote to remind myself that in order to play for my province and my country, it's not just about winning – it's about putting the effort in. I firmly believe this. I had some talent as a young rugby player, but my main achievement has been working hard and, as Roosevelt put it, 'striving valiantly'. There may have been others more talented than me or more strategic, but I put in the work. When I was a younger player, I would do visualisations, imagining myself as part of a Grand Slam-winning team, thinking about where I wanted to be next. I can confirm that the technique really works.

The other thing I've taken from the Roosevelt quotation is that when I'm in a tight corner, I ask myself the question, *How do you come back stronger from this? How do you take this bad situation and make it into something that'll spur you on to better things?*

My dad always told me that there was no greater honour than to be selected for the Lions. Donning that red jersey and crossing to the other side of the world to represent these islands would be the pinnacle of my playing career. As a child, I would ask for a Lions replica shirt every Christmas and I wore each one until it practically fell apart on me, so to sit here in Perth on the first stop of the 2025 Lions tour of Australia is almost surreal. Dad was right. It is the honour of a lifetime. For me, it's been a real pinch-yourself moment. Every now and then I stop and think just how special it is and how important it is not to take it for granted. Sometimes I can get so caught up in the moment that I need to take a step back and realise that this is what I've wanted to do since I was four years old and going to Wesley Minis with Dad. For my whole life, this was the summit of the mountain and now I'm really here.

The moment is all the sweeter because I missed out on the 2021 tour of South Africa due to a foot injury. I may have 'dared greatly', but in the end I failed. Recently, someone sent me a photo of myself in my red Lions strip, matching face mask on (it was during Covid), signing photos and shirts for the 2021 tour. I have no memory of that photo, probably because a week or so later I was out.

It's not easy to explain the impact of an injury on a player, or any athlete really. What might seem like a niggle to most people can end a career on the track or field. A pulled hamstring can mean months of physical therapy and rest; worse still is an anterior cruciate ligament (ACL) injury, which could have a player out for a year. I can guess what many readers might be thinking here: what about

Antoine Dupont's ACL injury in the Six Nations Ireland–France game earlier in 2025? He's a fantastic player, an icon of the game and a talisman to the French team; but his injury in the ruck was just an unfortunate rugby incident. I know that Fabien Galthié, the France head coach, took a different view, but I'm clear about it. It was a ruck in a fast professional game and there was no attempt to 'go after' Dupont's leg. I texted Antoine the day after the match to check in on him and he was very gracious in his reply: 'Thanks Andrew. Very unlucky, that's life. Thanks for the message.'

No player wants to go out with an injury like that – or any injury – but we're used to getting knocks and playing through them. There's a big emphasis in training on calves and hamstrings, because damage to them can keep you out for weeks or months, but less significant injuries are considered fairly normal. My AC (acromioclavicular) ligament, which holds your shoulder and collarbone together, is now completely torn away due to constant wear and tear, with the final blow coming in Scotland in the 2024 Six Nations. It was about fifteen minutes into the game and I was carrying the ball when I got tackled and I had an inkling that it was my AC ligament. However, with twenty-five minutes to go, I had to play on. It's such a common injury that you don't get much sympathy for it and I didn't. When I touch my shoulder now, it's almost as if I have a big bone sticking up where my ligament should be and I can actually grab it. There's no point in getting it fixed right now, because it'll probably happen again.

The next incident happened to me when I was playing Italy in the Six Nations and the syndesmosis ligament in my ankle (which connects the tibia and fibula) snapped. I think I got hit in a ruck and my body weight went over my ankle, with the unmistakeable popping sound that comes when the ligament snaps. Dan Sheehan happened to hear it and shouted, 'Are you okay?' 'I'm fine!' I shouted back, even though it was completely fecked, to use the medical term. I tried to ignore the pain and play on, but it was pointless. Frustrated, I had to come off, with David Kilcoyne replacing me. I had it strapped up at half time and later, when a scan confirmed the snapped ligament, I had it repaired surgically in Santry Sports Clinic. It's quite a simple procedure: they put a wire in your ankle to repair the ligament and after four weeks' rest, you're good to go, in theory at least. I had to go back to Leinster and spend eight weeks on the sidelines, missing out on Champions Cup and United Rugby Championship games, as well as the Six Nations. I returned to Leinster to play the semi-final of the URC in June, when we lost to the Bulls by just one point. Heartbreaking stuff.

My most gruesome injury happened during the first test against South Africa in 2024. We'd gone down to play two matches against the Boks. I've often dislocated my fingers, but I've never seen the inside of my hand before, and frankly, I don't ever want to see it again. It was a total freak accident: I'm not sure exactly how it happened but I think I caught my pinky in someone's shorts. I could feel the rip as it tore away from my hand but I wasn't prepared for the gore! I hit my finger against the side of my shorts and I managed to pop it back in, but I could see the bone in my finger and the ligaments. Play was still ongoing and as I looked at my hand in horror, I remember Calvin Nash yelling, 'Porter, get back in line!' So I kept defending until play stopped. I didn't want to let the team down by going off – I wanted to keep playing, but as my pinky was now hanging off my hand, I knew that I needed to go off at some point if I didn't want to lose it altogether. I can remember Jim McShane supporting my arm as I walked off the pitch and there's a great photo of me holding my hand, my face screwed up in pain and shock. I had the finger bandaged up and I ended up going back on. I needed surgery to fix it but, ultimately, it wasn't that big a deal. I went on to play in the second test, albeit well bandaged up.

Playing the Boks in their backyard is as tough as it gets.

We knew what was coming. Altitude. Power. Noise. The first test in Pretoria was brutal. They came out flying. The first scrum was like hitting a wall. We held, but it took everything we had. They scored early, but we stayed in it. I carried hard, tried to win the gain line and made a couple of key tackles. We lost that one narrowly, but it was agonising.

The second test, in Durban, was different. We adjusted to their style of play, played smarter and with a quicker ball. I remember one maul where we drove them back ten metres. That gave us belief. Jack Crowley kicked well including two drop goals, the last of which won it for us in the end, and Bundee was everywhere. We edged it 21–18. Series drawn. Not the clean sweep we wanted, but a huge step forward.

Playing in South Africa tests your soul. You feel every hit. But we stood up. I left that tour with bruises and pride. That meant something. The pinky injury was a symbol of just how tough it had been. Now, I look at the tiny scar that remains and it all comes flooding back.

Memories of the foot injury I picked up against Glasgow early in 2021 are as clear as if they happened yesterday. We were playing away on an Astro pitch, and I was running when I felt a sudden 'click'. I thought it was my boot, so I played on and it gradually became more and more painful.

Then I'd say it probably got stood on, because by the end of the match I was barely able to walk off the pitch. My stomach sank to my boots as I sat with the team medic, who gently examined my foot. 'I'd say you'll need an X-ray when you get back,' he said.

It's only an X-ray, I thought as I headed from the airport to St Vincent's Hospital A&E. *It might be nothing.* Thankfully, I drive an automatic car, so I didn't need to press the pedals with both feet, but it wasn't a nice journey. All the way into town and out along the coast road, I couldn't help thinking, *What if it's not nothing? What if you miss out on the Lions tour?* In these situations, you try to remain hopeful until you get the results, so I sat in the busy emergency room, watching the walking wounded and their worried relatives, thinking, *Some of these people are far worse off than me. It's going to be fine.*

The X-ray confirmed that my metatarsal on the outside of my foot was broken. I felt numb, in shock. I tried to put a brave face on it for the doctor, but I knew that my tour was over before it had even begun. I hobbled out to my car and sat behind the wheel, in bits. I'd grown up watching the Lions, thinking that one day I'd be there, on tour with the best of my contemporaries. Now, there was no chance I'd go. It was over. I can remember banging my head off the steering wheel in sheer frustration. I swore profusely then tried to compose myself for the drive home. I think Elaine had gone out for the night because the house was empty and I can remember getting home and sitting on the kitchen floor and crying my eyes out. I think I got through about half a bottle of whiskey: *I won't be playing for six weeks anyway,* I thought, *so I might as well drown my sorrows.*

When the news got out, so many people rallied round. Elaine, of course, Dad, my school friends … they all knew what a tough situation it was. I was heartbroken. At the time, I thought it was the be-all and end-all, but now that I have a child it kind of puts things into perspective. I can now see the bigger picture, even if at the time it felt as if the rug had been pulled from under me. I had got my hopes up so much about the tour that I just couldn't see beyond it.

For the 2025 Lions tour of Australia, I didn't let myself get ahead of myself. Even when the team was picked and I was selected, I thought, *Well, I still have games to play. I'm not going to pussyfoot around for Leinster just in case. I'm going to keep playing well for Leinster and once the season's finished, then I can think about the Lions.* I didn't want to think, *I'm not going to give my best because I don't want to get injured.*

Back in 2021, I didn't really have that perspective. A funny thing happens when you're seriously injured: you suddenly find that you're a bit of a spare part. You go to training, but you're not following the same regime as the others on the team, so you're on the sidelines, looking on. You're in the building, but it's as if you're a ghost. You're doing rehab on your own and going to the gym at different times, and for the medics and physios, the team is the priority because they'll have a match that week, so they fit you in when they can. It's not quite like being in isolation, but it's not a welcome feeling.

Then, I was still a tighthead prop, and even though I knew that I could play both sides of the scrum, tighthead was where I saw myself fitting in. So when Robin McBryde, the Leinster and Lions assistant coach, met me before the team flew off in 2021 and asked me what I'd think about moving back to loosehead, I wasn't sure about it. John Fogarty, the Irish scrum coach, had put this to me before. I thought that I was going well at tighthead and I knew that the adjustment would take time. Besides, I was in a terrible place and I kept thinking, *I worked really hard to get to this point. And now it's all gone.* I hadn't done anything to make it happen – it was an accident – but it cut really deep. I just wanted something to swallow me up; anything to get me through this feeling. I wasn't really listening when Rob continued, 'Look, Tadhg [Furlong, who plays tighthead] is obviously an incredible player and you're an incredible player: we want you on the pitch at the same time rather than when Tadhg's played sixty minutes and you just come on. We want to have the two of you on at the same time.'

As the team flew off to South Africa for the tour, I tried to adopt a positive mindset. With a pin in my foot to fix the fracture, I couldn't put any weight on it. I couldn't cycle or use an exercise bike, but I didn't want to lose condition, so I got a Nordic ski machine to keep up my fitness. I knew that my injury wouldn't last long but it felt like an age. Time seemed to slow to a crawl as I skied away and tried not to think about what I was missing. I couldn't bear to watch a single match of the tour: not because I was envious but because it made me think of what I was missing. Elaine watched every one of the matches and she was always encouraging me to watch with her, but I couldn't. 'I'm going for a walk,' I'd tell her, or 'I'm going to the gym.' Whatever I could do to get out of the house. Maybe this sounds like an overreaction, but when you've aimed for something for years and you miss out, you can't help but feel hard done by. I was gutted for Caelan Doris when he missed out on the 2025 Lions Tour with a shoulder injury because I know how that feels. And what certainty did I have that I'd ever be picked again?

Finally, I came around to accepting my fate. It was an

accident and there was nothing I could do to change that. But what I could do was to think hard about moving back to loosehead. Funnily enough, that injury helped me in the end, because it got me to where I am now. *Right,* I thought, *I'm going to use this time to get myself in the best shape I've been in and be the best loosehead that I can be.* I threw myself into the project and got myself to a place where I could be confident that I could just go and do it and not have any excuses as to why I wasn't starting or why I wasn't picked. I tried to literally cut out all the bullshit around me and go with a no-excuses kind of attitude. I'd just do the work in the early mornings in the gym and the late evenings at training. It was the end of the season then so I had a block of five weeks off and I spent that five weeks preparing for the season. When I set my mind on something, I just throw everything at it.

I sat out the summer and then I came back for Leinster in a game against Bulls and I scored a try. It felt unbelievable after the previous three months. As if a weight had been lifted off my shoulders. I almost didn't credit myself with having that tenacity, but I surprised myself. Some of that is due to the mentality of the professional sportsperson, but part of it is my own mentality. If I weren't as driven as I am, I wouldn't be playing rugby. I'd have picked something easier! It's a tough physical game that really takes its toll on the body. I'd say I feel sore about 60 per cent of the time from a combination of training and the knocks you get in matches. We're looked after really well by Leinster and Ireland, and they are careful not to overplay us, but it's just a fact of the modern game.

I can see now that in contrast to the World Cup quarter-finals in 2023, my attitude was very different. I kept training because I wanted to get back in and I knew that I hadn't done anything to cause this injury. It was bad luck more than anything. I would come back a better player, I'd thought. This was my chance. I didn't want to use my injury as an excuse – I almost wanted to excel at coming back from injury. *I can be the best injured person in my sport*, I thought to myself! You can't play rugby or sport in general unless you have a competitive streak in you. My competition was with myself. I was the main person I was trying to impress, if that makes sense.

And now, I'm sitting in a hotel room in Sydney, having scored a try in our match against the Queensland Reds. The feeling is really special, all the more so because during the Six Nations, the individual countries would have been trying to kill each other. On a Lions tour, you go from trying to take lumps out of each other to finding out that you all have the same goal. We might have different personalities, but we're all professional, we're all lucky enough to be doing something that we love doing and I'm blessed to be among the best of the best. Plus, we all have a job to do and that definitely sharpens the mind. Dad was right – it is the honour of a lifetime. It's everything I expected and more.

CHAPTER 8

SHOWING THE WAY

'Show me a successful individual and I'll show you someone who had real positive influences in his or her life. I don't care what you do for a living – if you do it well, I'm sure there was someone cheering you on or showing the way. A mentor.'

Denzel Washington

recently came across a photo of myself as a child coming out onto the pitch with the Leinster captain, none other than Leo Cullen. I was holding his hand going out for the game, and now Leo is my coach and one of many incredible mentors I've had in my life and in my career.

My first and most important mentor was my dad. He encouraged me not only on the pitch at Old Wesley but also in life. It wasn't so much what he said but what he did. The way he carried himself in life was with dignity, humour and a cast-iron work ethic. With Dad, it wasn't hard to learn how to be a decent human being. He also wasn't afraid to tell me how to behave on the rugby pitch.

But there's no way I'd be where I am now without those who helped me on my way at various stages. As Denzel Washington says, there were people who showed me the way, like my first coach in St Andrew's, Mr Jones, or Cian Healy, who I looked up to so much when I started in Leinster. There were people who encouraged me: John Fogarty, who also gave me my first knock-back (with good reason), Stuart Lancaster, Leo Cullen, Andy Farrell – they knew instinctively how to get the best out of me, but, more important, how to instil confidence in me. In my experience, positive encouragement does far more to help a player than making them afraid of making a mistake. Andy Farrell has said that he encourages players to be themselves and I think that's the best possible way to play.

Liam Griffin was appointed by our Irish team manager, Mick Kearney, to mentor me and I'll always be grateful to him for introducing me to Stoicism and to concepts that made a lot of sense to me. Liam was helping me to look at my personal development outside rugby and he gave me a few books to read, one of which was Ryan Holiday's *The Obstacle is the Way*, which really struck a chord with me. Holiday has become famous for interpreting the Stoic way and for making it popular and accessible. Until reading Holiday, I hadn't realised that the original works of Marcus Aurelius and philosophers like Seneca and Epictetus were still incredibly relevant.

The 'virtuous ways' of the Stoics are a simple blueprint

for living well. Concepts like *memento mori* really struck home with me. Literally translated, it means, 'remember death' – but what it means in reality is that we're all going to die one day, so it's important to make every day count. It doesn't mean we should go around thinking about dying; we should simply live with the awareness that our time on earth is finite, so we need to make the most of it. I think this would have made a great deal of sense to Mum – and, maybe without realising it, she lived her life in just this way.

The other thing that hit home for me was the way in which Stoicism focuses on managing the emotions, something that's really important for sports people. In my sport, emotions are always going to run high, because that's the nature of the game. It's a high-intensity sport. I think I bring a lot of energy and aggression to the scrum, but sometimes that can result in decisions not going my way. That's when I have to be stoic, because getting upset about it won't change the decision – it'll only make me upset and I won't play well. I can remember telling RTÉ's Neil Treacy earlier this year, 'I've been through [games] where I've spent nearly the whole game thinking: "I've been taken for a ride by the ref here" but it doesn't really get you anywhere. It's trying to have that mental calmness when things are going for you and against you.' That's the key –

you need to apply that mental stoicism whether you're winning or losing.

I haven't always managed to implement this one, but I keep trying. I remember the World Cup quarter-final against New Zealand really challenged me. When a couple of decisions didn't go my way, I did lose it a bit. I remember telling a few pundits the same thing:

> A lot of the time you know you're in the wrong when a penalty is given against you, but [in] the 50/50 calls where you feel a bit hard done by, it's really tough not to get worked up about it. I could even feel that in the New Zealand game, in the quarter-final, my blood was honestly boiling after a while because I just felt like I had been hard done by.

That was partly why I found coming to terms with that loss so difficult, because I hadn't managed my emotions on that occasion and I'd paid the price.

I can also remember when we played Wales in 2024 and I got a lot of stick for tossing Gareth Thomas's boot away when he lost it in the scrum. There was a bit of a scuffle afterwards, but I just wanted to get the boot out of the way so that it wouldn't interfere with play or trip someone up, and because I thought it was funny! I wasn't annoyed about it. But lots of commentators thought it should be a yellow card. It's difficult when you're in the front row and you have that responsibility – that if a decision doesn't go your way, it could tip the balance in favour of the other team. The toughest situations are the 50/50 calls that don't work out in your favour, particularly when the match hangs in the balance. All the more reason not to lose it: it won't make any difference to the outcome.

In 2016, my first year in the Leinster set-up, Stuart Lancaster came in as coach and he was great for instilling confidence in me. He said, 'Look, you've got the size and the skills: it's the small percentages that you need to just keep improving on. You have the potential to be a great prop and to go on and play for Leinster, Ireland and the Lions.' That really spurred me on and he gave me tangible goals to aim for – fortunately, because the Leinster senior set-up was completely different from the under-20s. I was in the house with the big dogs and the level was so much higher. It was almost a different game. I had been playing 80 minutes for the under-20s at 130 kg and yet I struggled to get through Stu's training sessions at Leinster. Ironically, I had to lose a bit of weight so that I could be more mobile around the park. Being big had got me by until now, but under Stu's guidance, I knew that I needed to be a good ball player as well. I had to work on my fitness and my mobility and on building my engine.

Stu was famous for his tough training sessions. They were almost tougher than the games. The idea was that after one of his sessions, the game would seem easy, but it was a steep learning curve for me. Tuesday was fondly known as Stu's Day. We'd be tiptoeing into the day, wondering just how tough the session was going to be. We'd have our team meeting and at the end, Stu would say, 'Okay, let's bring the oxygen tanks today, boys.' That's when we knew we were in for a session!

Stu would have us playing on one end of the pitch and then he'd blow a whistle and we'd have to sprint down the length of the pitch to the other end, play down there for a bit, before he'd blow the whistle again. We were basically doing lengths of the pitch while also playing rugby, so the conditioning work was built in. We weren't just running for the sake of running, which I never liked. If you're being timed or running for a certain number of seconds, it always feels much longer. If we were on the ball, it was easy to forget just how bolloxed we all were.

We also knew that if we'd worked hard, it was money in the bank for the weekend matches. If you're fit, you can lean on that and you're much more confident going into games. Under Stu's guidance, I grew in confidence and in mental stature.

Leo Cullen is also amazing for encouraging the players. He's always been in my corner. For a start, he saw the potential in me to give me a contract at Leinster – that goes a long way. When you have coaches backing you, bigging you up and filling you with confidence, it gives you the courage to reach your full potential. He's a tremendous influence in the building and, of course, takes the lead in team selection, but he lets the individual coaches do their thing. Leo is always around, but Jacques Nienaber has been a huge influence on us this year, introducing the infamous Springboks blitz defence to the team. Hard work, but with proven results.

I'm not the only one to fear failure, but I also know that that very fear can cause you to tighten up, to overthink and ultimately to fail. It's one of life's ironies. I remember talking to Cian Healy about it. I'd always looked up to Cian because he'd been playing since before I came into Leinster. Playing with someone you idolise is a bit strange, but Cian was always the type of person to take you under his wing and teach you and talk to you. The fact that he was very much a no-bullshit guy and really easy-going helped. I think he understood exactly what it was like as a novice and the anxieties about being a younger player in a big team. He was incredible in terms of giving me confidence and telling me not to worry about it too much. At the time I can remember thinking, *How? It's easy for you to say that!* But Cian helped me to understand that I hadn't been picked by the coaches for no reason. 'You're here because, obviously, you're good enough,' he would often say. He was brilliant at explaining that to me and giving me confidence. He's been doing that since I began and now he's just retired. He's been an amazing mentor to me. We'll all miss him.

My first ever scrum coach in the Ireland squad was Greg Feek and he taught me a lot. He invited me in to see him in Clonskeagh House to chat, even though I hadn't got my Ireland cap at that stage. He must have seen something in me, so he gave me a path to follow to improve my prospects as a tighthead, and a bit of structure too. He taught me the essentials and he taught me well. He's now been replaced by John Fogarty – Foggy – who's a great guy, incredible craic, a great operator who lifts the morale of the team, but I'll always remember Greg because of the interest he took in me and the time he gave to helping me improve.

As a young player, I had a bit of a chip on my shoulder because I didn't go to a big rugby school. I felt that I had to work a bit harder to get noticed. The guys from the big rugby schools would come in and they would already be known. I used to think that maybe the coaches would look at them and assume they knew what they were doing, but then I'd see that they had the weight of expectation on their shoulders. I was free to just get on with it and to adapt. A lot of players have come and gone, thinking that they can be the same player that they were coming in, not changing to meet the demands of professional sport. My start in St Andrew's meant that I was a bit more flexible, but without Cian and players like Johnny Sexton and Tadhg Furlong to set me straight, I'm not sure I'd have learned the ropes as quickly. Johnny in particular was a role model. I was amazed by his work ethic and attention to detail. He was the standard-driver for the team and the players, helping to get the extra percentage out of the team. Caelan Doris is an incredible leader for both Leinster and Ireland. He's a very intelligent player and person and I admire him for the way he carries himself. He's a great athlete and a great mate as well.

One of the biggest learning curves for me was being a youngster in this room full of grown-ups. You think you have to project this image that you belong and you're not in awe of everyone, but of course, at team meetings there are people in the room you can't believe you're sharing the same space with. It was a delicate balance between respecting their experience and professionalism and showing them what you can do. I can't say I always got the balance right.

I can remember one time the ball was kicked and I was running back and I was blocking Seán O'Brien. No big deal, but I might have done that a couple of times in the session, and it was beginning to get on his nerves. The final time I blocked him would be my last, because he grabbed me by the collar, thumped me and split my lip open. I swung a few punches as well, but into thin air. I had to go down to St Vincent's to get stitched up. Lesson learned. Seánie is coaching in Leinster these days and we laugh about it now. Sometimes mentoring can take different forms!

The same went for Johnny Sexton when I was on the under-20s team. Since he was one of the most respected players in the world, I was a bit afraid of him at the start. We were playing against the senior team in training, which is an essential part of bringing younger players along. I was determined to prove my worth, as was everyone else, and with the young bucks facing the big guys, things got a bit heated. In this particular session, I remember the tension building as we played: the senior team were getting ratty with the juniors snapping at their heels, and the juniors were getting impatient. I can't remember how it happened, but somehow or another, I managed to get Johnny Sexton on the ground with his jersey over his face.

He was on the ground, kit pulled up over his head, while I was on him, holding him down. He swung blindly into thin air while yours truly held on to him for dear life. I can still remember thinking, *This is an icon of the Irish rugby team. Do. Not. Hit. Him.* I knew that I couldn't touch him, so instead I hung on to him until one of the coaches sprinted over to break it up.

I knew better than to let things escalate further and to his credit, Johnny got up and we got on with the game, not a bad word exchanged. Handbags, rather than anything reckless or deliberate. Later, we'd talk about it and sort it out. As long as you're not being stupid, it's considered normal to go toe-to-toe during training. As young players, we'd try to wind up the older lads and get under their skin a bit, but we knew where the line was and we were wise enough not to cross it. We respected their experience and superior skills. This is rugby, not ice hockey, where the enforcer tries to rack up the most penalty minutes by going after an opponent. It's a team sport.

The 2023 Grand Slam match against England in the Aviva Stadium was Johnny's last Six Nations match, and we were desperate to send him off with a win. The first half was tense, with Owen Farrell scoring two penalties early on as England nudged ahead. We lost Caelan Doris and Dan Sheehan early to injury, then England went down to fourteen men after Freddie Steward's red card. He'd made contact with Hugo Keenan's head and Hugo had gone off with suspected concussion. It was a controversial decision, but it changed the game. We regrouped at half-time and came out sharper. Dan came back on and scored a brilliant try off a loop play. I remember hitting a ruck just before that, clearing space for Jamison Gibson-Park to get the ball away. Then Robbie Henshaw powered over and Dan got his second. England kept coming, but we held firm. I was blowing hard in the last ten minutes. Every carry felt heavier, every tackle more important. When the whistle went, I looked up and saw the crowd erupt. We'd done it. A Grand Slam in Dublin. That night we celebrated properly. It was emotional. Johnny's last Six Nations game, a perfect send-off. I felt proud of the group, proud of the journey. That campaign was one of the best of my life.

Of course, because it had been so special, we really celebrated, and thanks to the wonders of social media, the festivities were out there for everyone to see. We were probably on day three of celebrating when someone had the bright idea to 'kidnap' some of the team's dads and take them into town for a few pints. I remember barging into Hugo Keenan's house when his dad was in the middle of a business meeting, lifting him out of the chair and taking him with us on the bus into town. I seem to remember that Garry Ringrose's dad was another willing victim. I suppose that's what we'll look back on in a few years. You create a special bond with your teammates because you go through a lot together, and it's fantastic to have memories to look back on and to laugh at. And it's great to see the fans' feedback or comments on the videos. I seem to remember a lot of ironic 'incredible horseplay' comments, which I thought was hilarious. I love it when people are involved enough to enjoy it with us and to have a bit of craic. It's impossible to over-estimate Johnny's contribution to the team and how much he'll be missed. He's joined the Lions as an assistant coach and is already applying that brilliant strategic brain of his to the team.

Tadhg Furlong was ahead of me on the Leinster and Ireland teams and he's a terrific player and a great mentor in the sense that he showed me how it was done. I wanted to get to his level, so that was something for me to strive for. Tadhg is the kind of rugby player I needed to be. His is the standard of play I needed to aim for. With Tadhg, I could learn and turn my raw ability into actual skill.

The second game of the Six Nations championship in 2018 was my personal baptism of fire. The team was on a high, having beaten France in the 81st minute with Johnny's incredible drop goal from the French half. This time we were playing Italy and I was on the bench. You always think that when the moment comes you'll be ready, but when Tadhg pulled up after three minutes with a tight hamstring, I was not. My first thought was *Shit, I have to play seventy-seven whole minutes in my first Six Nations game.* But before I knew it, I was on, thrown into the game with no time to be nervous or, crucially, to overthink things. Usually, I'd be on the bench imagining what I'd do and thinking, *Okay, just don't go near the ball and you won't drop it or make a mistake.* Now, I didn't have time to think of that because I was just thrown into the game, and because I wasn't getting in my own way, I played quite well – to my own surprise! I started in the next two games against Wales and Scotland, and it was another big step up in my game.

As a young player, you're always worried about your performance. If you're not 'on it', you're obviously not going to be there for that long. You need to be at the top of your game. The thing is, when you think about mistakes too much or you're trying to over-analyse things, it can really affect your play. I wasn't a very confident player at the start of my career and I can still remember heading into camp in the early days, my stomach in a knot of anxiety. Joe Schmidt was the coach at the time and I had him to thank for giving me my very first cap. He saw the potential in me and I'm incredibly grateful for that. He was an exacting coach, and a true innovator in terms of plays, which were always very well thought out. His technical ability was second to none and his attention to detail exceptional. He's done amazing work with the Wallabies, and Conor Murray was right when he wrote in the *Irish Times* that it would be a mistake to underestimate any team coached by him. The third test of the 2025 Lions series certainly proved that.

Because I was a rookie, I was excited to be going to camp in Carton House, but almost dreading it at the same time: I was burnt out from overthinking, from analysing every player's role so that I wouldn't mess up. It was the opposite feeling to the one I have now: any time I'm heading into camp, Elaine will joke, 'Oh, you're delighted to be leaving me now, aren't you?' Now, I'm practically skipping out the door. It's the experience that counts, I think.

Andy Farrell is now our coach and I think what makes Andy such a special leader is that he's been through it all himself. He's been a professional rugby player, so I think he understands what players are going through off the pitch as well as on. He's also been brilliant at creating a family atmosphere around the team. He knows that players don't want to be always 'on', thinking about rugby the whole time, so his approach is that we get our work done to a high standard and then we can switch off and enjoy our lives outside rugby. With Andy, our entire identities aren't dependent on rugby and that might seem counter-intuitive in today's professional atmosphere, but it creates much better balance and a real sense of lightness in the dressing room. We obviously play to win, but we also play because we love doing what we do. It makes it so much easier when you love your job and you like coming in to do it.

And as a family man, Faz gets the fact that the players have families at home who they are missing and he brings them into the fold as much as he can. There are always functions after matches for the whole family and it creates a fantastic atmosphere. Bringing my newborn son to the Lions gathering in the Aviva Stadium was incredibly special to me and Elaine. That positive culture comes from the top down and it makes it a great deal of fun to go in to work. We're there because we want to be, because we understand what an incredible privilege it is to represent our country, and because we also know that we're playing with a real positivity.

Andy is also a great speaker and his team talks are always inspiring. He made us a bit emotional when we first came together as Lions in Dublin for the 2025 training camp. He described ringing Finlay Bealham and telling him he had made it onto the plane to Australia to replace the injured Zander Fagerson. Finlay had cried tears of emotion and joy (even though he claimed he didn't!). 'That's it right there, lads,' Faz said. 'I know we all take the piss out of one another, but that's what it should mean to be a British and Irish Lion.' We all had a good laugh at that. 'This is the best time of your life. Give all of yourself to this team, absolutely every single ounce of you. It's about genuinely caring for one another and enjoying the experience that we're going to have over the next eight weeks.' That's exactly what we intended to do. That's great leadership.

It goes without saying that as players, we always want to get better, but not just for our own sakes. We want to improve as a unit as well as individually. We mentor each other and the younger players so that we continue to improve. If you can pour your knowledge into someone else, hopefully they can fulfil their potential as a professional rugby player just as we did. For example, we often discuss the scrums because it's such a technical part of the game and so positioning-specific. We come up against all kinds of different issues that require us to come up with different solutions. We could be facing different sizes of tightheads – taller ones, smaller ones who can get down low – so we constantly have to adjust and tailor our knowledge.

We don't need to sit down and have a summit meeting, but we will often stop each other in the corridor or dressing room to ask a question or discuss an issue: I think in the office world they're called standing meetings. If you struggled in a game and you want to get better, you want to get past it, you want to be able to deal with it in the next game so it doesn't happen again, you discuss it with your teammates and coaches. For example, in Leinster at the moment, I'm scrumming against Rabah Slimani, the incredibly accomplished French tighthead, and we'd often chat about what each of us does against the other. We'd ask questions like 'What would you hate a loosehead doing to you in a scrum? What would a loosehead do to make your job incredibly easy (so I won't do it!)?' These kinds of questions keep you learning and improving. That's the thing with mentors: they are there not to tell you what to do but to help you to keep learning. As the proverb says: 'A wise man never knows all. Only a fool knows everything.'

You are always a work in progress, no matter what kind of job you do in life. I know that as a loosehead prop, I might have a ton of experience, but if I'm not willing to be flexible in my approach, to keep learning and adapting, I won't improve. The dictionary definition of a mentor is 'someone who teaches or gives help and advice to a less experienced and often younger person', but I think that you can continue to be mentored throughout your professional life, no matter how experienced you are. One of my biggest mentors recently has been my friend Josh Percival. We've been going through the journey of trying to set up our gym together and I've learned such a lot from him. He's clued in, organised and business-minded. He has master's degrees in nutrition, and strength and conditioning, and with my long experience in the elite sports area, we complement each other well. Josh lost his dad a few years ago, so we both know what it's like to lose someone really important to us.

My cousin, Rob Priestman, has been a huge influence on me – not just in sport, but in life beyond it. Like me, he was a bit of a messer in school, but through sheer hard work and focus he's built a successful career and life. Rob has helped me develop a business mindset and shown me the importance of thinking beyond rugby. His journey has inspired me to challenge myself, step outside of my comfort zone, and prepare for what comes after the game.

Mentoring is particularly useful for younger players, but even though I've been in the game for almost ten years now as a professional, I am still keen to learn and to evolve. That's the key: if you think you know it all, you most definitely don't. As Darwin said, 'Ignorance more frequently begets confidence than does knowledge.' The best players, in my opinion, are those who wear their knowledge lightly, who are willing to share it with others and who recognise that no matter how much they know, there is always something new to learn.

CHAPTER 9

WINNER TAKES ALL

'The impediment to action advances action. What stands in the way becomes the way.'

Marcus Aurelius, **Meditations**

There are some days you will never forget, some special memories that will live in your mind forever. St Patrick's Day 2018 is one such day. The Six Nations championship had gone well for us. We began the campaign with a tight win against France, 15–13, but then enjoyed a comfortable win against Italy (56–19) and a less comfortable but still decent ten-point win over Wales, then a twenty-point win over Scotland. We now found ourselves up against England in our bid to win the Triple Crown and the Grand Slam. England were hoping to become the first team to win three Triple Crowns in a row, so there was a lot at stake for both teams. England also had home ground advantage at Twickenham and hadn't been beaten there in six years. The Irish fans were out in force and 'The Fields of Athenry' was being belted out through the falling snow. The atmosphere in the stadium was immense.

The first half was electric. Garry Ringrose scored early, then CJ Stander crashed over and Jacob Stockdale chipped and chased for a brilliant try. We were 21–5 up at the break. In the second half England were starting to come back and the crowd was getting louder. I came on for Tadhg Furlong around the 65-minute mark. My first scrum was just inside our 10-metre line. I focused on my bind, stayed low and we held firm. I hit a couple of rucks hard and made a tackle on Mako Vunipola that rattled me. Some things didn't go our way – Peter O'Mahony was sent to the sin bin for collapsing a maul, Bundee Aki went off injured and Johnny Sexton followed. England scored another try with fifteen minutes to go, but we held on. When the whistle blew, I looked around and saw the lads jumping, hugging, shouting. We'd done it. A Grand Slam, and only the third Irish team to do it. Fireworks and champagne bottles exploded in unison as we celebrated the win.

What I remember best about that day is climbing into the stands to meet my dad after we did our lap of honour, knowing just how much it meant to him. The beer flowed in the dressing room and the songs did too. Later, in response to a question about motivation,

I apparently said that my motivators were my family, my girlfriend and my dog! Nothing wrong with wanting to do well for those you love. That's always been my motivation, to make them proud.

The youngsters among the team headed out into town after the dressing-room celebrations and I remember someone coming back with a real policeman's helmet! I have no idea how that happened. We returned to Dublin in the thick of the Beast from the East, to find the country covered in a thick blanket of snow and our homecoming in the Aviva cancelled. We did gather with our families in the Shelbourne Hotel, though, and it was a real family occasion. I love the family atmosphere in rugby and the sense that we were celebrating a win for more than just ourselves. To me, that's always been a really important motivator.

People often ask me what winning feels like and it's a good question. The emotions are probably not what people expect. Of course, there's elation, often there's exhaustion after a tough match, and sometimes there's sheer relief that you've got through without making mistakes or letting your teammates down. Quite often there's been an internal battle to get to the finish line and you can feel too wrecked to enjoy yourself. But other times, you just want to let rip! So much of the game is about keeping calm mentally, keeping your emotions in check so that you can play well, so when we get the chance, we really want to celebrate.

When you win there's that moment of joy, but there's also the relief that comes with it, when everything that you've worked so hard for becomes a reality. Sir John Kirwan is someone who knows all about this. He played for the All Blacks between the mid-1980s and mid-1990s and is one of the iconic figures in the game as well as being a brilliant campaigner for mental health. His most famous moment is probably his 70-metre run up the field against Italy in the very first World Cup in 1987, scoring a try after neatly sidestepping the Italian opposition. It's still impressive today, even more so because, as he happily admitted, they didn't train. This seems incredible to me, who trains morning, noon and night. What he then revealed, though, told me a lot about determination. Obviously, he began life as an amateur, so his day job was helping his dad out in his butcher's shop. One day, a local rugby league player came into the shop and invited Kirwan to try out his speed and his sidestepping skills by running through an avenue of trees on a local street. The first time, he dodged the first tree, but hit the second head on. For the next ten months, he ran up that street until he could side-step each and every tree. And when

New Zealand won, he said, 'I remember feeling more relief than celebration that we hadn't let our ancestors down.'

This resonates with me because my primary emotion when I win is the sense of a weight being lifted off my shoulders, that I haven't let my teammates down, or the country. It's interesting that even though I'm playing in the professional era, when we are constantly told 'there's so much at stake', the emotions are the same as John's. He's a person I really admire because of his openness in talking about the depression he had throughout his career: the work he's done in mental health in New Zealand is incredible. I hope to be as effective as he is as a campaigner.

Rugby is a complete team sport and it requires you to think with a collective mindset. Looking out for number one isn't an option. In the past I've met people who haven't made it on a team and sometimes it's because they haven't bought into that. They might not have been ready to commit to that way of thinking. Some players might get more outside focus than others but you can't be an egotistical team member. You have to be humble as a person. Rugby has given me so much – a job and a passion, but it's also given me tools for life, if that doesn't sound too grandiose. You aren't doing your best just for yourself, but for others too, and that's really important. You're grounded by that mentality and encouraged to believe that everyone is equal. At least, in my club anyway! Leinster is my home, it's the club I grew up watching and I never wanted to play for anyone else.

I didn't think I'd play in my first Six Nations game in only my second season in Leinster. I didn't see that it would happen that quickly. But once I'd gone through my baptism of fire, I began to play more often and with more confidence. I knew that I was very much a small fish surrounded by quality players, but crucially, being in games regularly began to work for me. it. If I came up short I could say to myself, *It's not as if I didn't give it my all.*

That's the interesting thing about winning and losing, I think, something we talk a lot about with the team's sports psychologists. First of all, losing is part of life; being afraid of losing is not the same as wanting to win. Being afraid of losing means that you'll often make mistakes and not play with any kind of flair; wanting to win can really spur you on, but, as I know, winning isn't everything. You have to deal with the pressure of expectation, which we learned all about in the 2023 World Cup. Then there's the assumption that we're expecting to win all around us, which we're not. I think that's often projected onto us as players; but our only goal is to play well.

Some losses sting more than others, though. In the 2023

Getting tackled in my first Leinster senior game against Treviso

With James Ryan following our international debuts in New Jersey

Grand Slam and Triple Crown winners, 2018

Getting tackled by Owen Farrell, left, and Manu Tuilagi during the
Six Nations final match in 2023

Getting stuck into a maul against Scarlets during a URC match in 2021

Playing through the pandemic: Rory O'Loughlin, me, Garry Ringrose and James Tracy with the Guinness PRO14 trophy in an empty Aviva 2020

Scoring my first try against the All Blacks in New Zealand, 2022

Elaine tries to console me, with Leigh on the right, after the
2023 Rugby World Cup quarter-final match in Paris

My first test match as a 2025 British and Irish Lion
against the Wallabies in Brisbane

Celebrating winning the series

Taking part in the Tackle Your Feelings campaign, run by Rugby Players Ireland

Working with Movember, who fund programmes that support men's physical and mental health

The Covid mask I designed for the Irish Cancer Society

Above: Starting a new chapter with my beautiful bride, Elaine

Left: From the pitch to parenthood: A special moment with Elaine and baby Max at Lions training

Where it began…

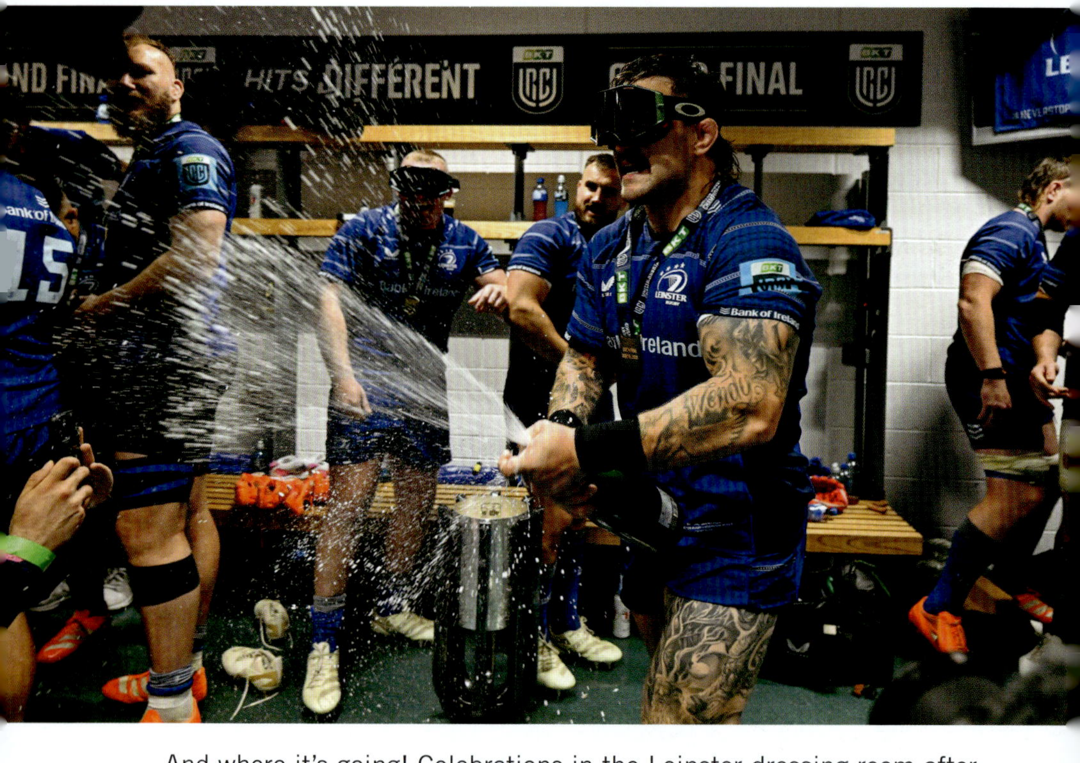

And where it's going! Celebrations in the Leinster dressing room after winning the URC, 2025

Champions Cup season, we were outplayed by a strong La Rochelle team led by Ronan O'Gara – and he's not called 'a wily old fox' for nothing. I still think about that loss. We'd started like a train, with three tries in the first twenty minutes. I remember hitting a cleanout that helped set up Jimmy O'Brien's score. The crowd was roaring. We were 17–0 up and flying. But La Rochelle didn't panic. They slowed the game down, kept the ball and started to claw their way back. I could feel the shift as their power game started to bite. Will Skelton and Grégory Alldritt were relentless. We went in at half-time still ahead but the momentum had changed. In the second half, we couldn't get out of our half. I gave away a penalty at a scrum that led to a lineout and then a maul try. We were under pressure and couldn't find a way to swing it back. When they scored the winner with minutes to go, it was gutting. We had one last chance but lost the lineout. The final whistle blew and there was silence. We'd let it slip on home turf.

After the match, ROG said, 'There were one or two guys sulking at 12–7 down at half-time but we knew we're a second-half team. We knew that the last twenty minutes was where we could get them.' And they did. There's really no good word for it. As to what went wrong, well, it's easy to look back and think, oh, we should have done this, we should have done that, but they were just the better team on the day, in spite of Johnny's six penalties. They stopped us making tries and the result was a hard pill to swallow. Losses like that stick with you. I think they have to, for you to excel and to be a kick up the backside for you, because you don't want to have those feelings. It's one of the worst feelings ever, doing so well in the season and then, when it matters, not coming back with the silverware. And being at home in front of the fans, that hurt.

When the 2025 encounter came around, we'd been waiting for a long time. La Rochelle had beaten us twice in finals. This time it was the semi-final of the Champions Cup in Dublin. We weren't going to let it slip. From the first whistle we were on it. I remember the first scrum: we got the nudge and that set the tone. Jamison was sharp. Hugo was electric. I carried off a lineout in their 22 and we built pressure. Sheehan scored off a maul and the place erupted. They came back, of course – they always do – but we stayed composed. I made a key turnover just before half-time that stopped a scoring chance. In the second half we pulled away. Ringrose finished a brilliant move and we closed it out. Final score 27–16. The roar at full-time was like nothing I've heard. It was all the more special because it happened in Dublin, in knockout rugby.

Going into the 2022 tour of New Zealand, I knew that we were pretty strong. We'd beaten the All Blacks in

Dublin the previous November, but were we strong enough to beat the All Blacks on their home turf? We certainly felt we could, but we knew that it was going to be tough. There was a cloud of uncertainty hanging over us, the weight of the fact that no Irish team had won down there before.

The first test match was in Auckland's legendary Eden Park, where the All Blacks had an unbeaten run of 46 games over 28 years. We lost the first test fairly resoundingly, in fact so resoundingly that many pundits wrote us off, but the 42–19 scoreline didn't reflect our ability, we knew that. We'd started the game so strongly with Keith Earls' try, but then the Kiwis began to exert a huge amount of pressure, filleting us fairly quickly with four tries before half-time. I can clearly remember one guy (I can't remember who) grabbing hold of my shirt and me bashing his hand away in frustration. In spite of another couple of tries in the second half, we were frustrated with our performance. Arguably, we were unlucky in having a couple of tries held up and I like to think that the scoreline flattered them a bit in the first game. But when our talisman, Johnny Sexton, went off with a suspected concussion, that really unsettled us. It was a frustrating game as we had had some wonderful passages of play, and two more tries from Ringrose and Bundee, but it was New Zealand's night. I can remember Alan Quinlan saying that the New Zealand performance was incredibly aggressive, and it was. Payback for the loss in Dublin.

That's what makes losing tough, I think: sometimes you'll have given everything and you'll still lose. There's a sense of unfairness about that, but as Brian O'Driscoll said, you just have to suck it up. There is no point in ruminating over past failures – you learn from your mistakes and you move on. So, on the Monday after that loss, we sat around on the pitch in training and had some open and honest conversations about what had happened in the first test and what we'd need to work on in the second test in order to win. You can't change things physically in the space of one week, so we discussed tactics, why the tries had been held up and what we might do differently. We hadn't played together since the Six Nations, so we knew that we were a bit rusty, but we also knew that we weren't miles off the pace. We'd had some good plays in the first match and played some good rugby, so there was the potential there to improve.

In Dunedin, we were going in with a point to prove. There was the usual commentary in the media about needing to change things up, but the same team faced them the second time around, apart from Mack Hansen, who was the substitute for Keith Earls. It's a cliché to talk about gladiators, but walking out through that tunnel into the stadium really was like being in the Colosseum, waiting for the lions to come out! The Dunedin stadium is covered – thankfully, because it was freezing and rainy – so the roar of the crowd was deafening. The Kiwis are passionate supporters of their team so the atmosphere was fevered. However, unlike in the previous match, the All Blacks didn't succeed in their game plan of lulling us into a false sense of security and then blasting us with their attacking game. We were straight out of the starting blocks and, crucially, sustained that energy in spite of the All Blacks' response. I almost can't remember the first try I scored, only three minutes into the game, but I can remember Mack Hansen had a good carry to the right-hand corner and then the ball got shifted out and came to Johnny. I thought that I was playing a running line, nearly a blocking line off Johnny, but then Johnny passed me the ball and the line was just there. I pushed forward and thumped the ball to the ground. The elation was something else.

We kept our composure then and succeeded in rattling the All Blacks, as two Kiwi yellow cards were followed by a red. With New Zealand down to 13 men, we had the advantage. I was raging when the ball slipped through my legs on our line for New Zealand to score. And all this before half-time. Thankfully, I scored again in the second half: I think we were close to the try line and Tadhg Beirne made a good break. I made one of my signature moves from a few inches out to get over the line. Some players score from twenty metres out, but not me: I'm more of a face-in-the-mud guy!

Then we stopped two New Zealand breaks to score two penalties. My future Leinster teammate Jordie Barrett set up a last-minute try by the All Blacks, just a little too late to affect the final scoreline. By the time Joey Carbery kicked the ball into the stands in the 80th minute the score was 23–12. It was an incredible feeling to win; to be the first Irish team to do so on New Zealand soil felt even sweeter. It was so emotional creating a bit of history. And I was certainly feeling emotional when Sky Sports interviewed me after the match, and I was so excited I dropped the f-bomb on live TV. The lads gave me a bit of slagging about that, but nothing could take away from that special day.

But your attention shifts pretty quickly to the next game. Sure, we'd won this, but we hadn't actually 'won' anything. The series was level and we needed to win the next match to properly win the series. I said to one journalist, 'We've created a bit of history today but the job's not done. All that matters is next week now. It'll be even sweeter if we can pull off the win next week as well.'

After the third test in Wellington, I can still remember

Andy saying that the most pleasing thing was that we kept our composure when they came back at us. We had laid down an early marker with tries from Josh van der Flier and Hugo Keenan and were 22–3 up at half time, but in the second half New Zealand came thundering back, with two tries in quick succession. I can still remember Will Jordan sprinting the length of the field to score a try for New Zealand – all we could do was look on in disbelief. Tadhg Beirne was a hero in defence and Rob Herring's 64th-minute try, coming away from the back of a maul and driving though the All Blacks' defence, was inspired.

The other thing I can remember from that final test was my clash of heads with Brodie Retallick, which earned me a yellow card. Brodie was carrying the ball when I went in for the tackle and because we were so close, I hadn't had time to get down to the ball, so we clashed heads instead. Off I went to the sin bin for ten minutes. Thankfully, Cian Healy came on for me, a guy who is so experienced: he made sure that they didn't put three tries past us while I was serving my sentence. There's nothing worse as a player than feeling you've let your teammates down but Cian made sure that didn't happen. I only learned that Brodie's cheekbone was broken after the match. I sent him a message to see if he was okay and he was very understanding. He knew that it wasn't malicious and that accidents can happen.

When the final whistle blew, with the scoreline at 32–22, we'd won. No wonder Peter O'Mahony was in tears at the end of that match: you can see how much it meant to him. It was hugely emotional. It felt amazing, and to do it together as a team – that was what made it really special. The overwhelming feeling of being able to do it with your teammates, and your mates at the end of the day, who you go through so much with, you train incredibly hard with, you spend so much time together – winning is one of those feelings that's incredibly hard to replicate but it means so much. The wins are incredible highs but the losses are incredible lows too: because you've worked so hard as a team, to come up short isn't just a case of individual disappointment: it's shared by the whole team.

That's the thing about rugby: it's a complete team sport. I couldn't imagine what it would be like to play an individual sport, because team sports require a very different mindset. Our battles are with our own minds but we also work really hard at thinking collectively. In individual sports, you can be exposed more and the work that you haven't done or your flaws, I'd say, are highlighted more, but in team sports, you have individuals who are obviously good in their roles, or their position, but it's having 15 or 23 people working together that counts. You have a team of great individuals, but it's what that team is together that makes the difference: everyone's skills and everyone's strengths all complement each other. We don't have to love each other as personalities but as players.

In every team I've been a part of, I don't think it's worked or the team is as good as it can be unless there's a good connection off the pitch. Not everyone can be best mates, but there's an overall sense of being together and trusting each other as professionals. You would trust that people are going to show up fully on the day, whether it's in training or in a game, to keep pushing the standards and to make sure the team gets better. We learn this right from the beginning, when it's not a profession, but when we all want to give our best for the team. Now, as professionals, we still want to give our best, but there are bigger consequences if you're not on your game or not taking it as seriously as everyone else. It's a truism to say that a chain is only as strong as its weakest link – it is. If you have fifteen men or women giving it their all and one of you is throwing the machine out of kilter, it's not going to work. All the parts need to work well together. Rugby is very much the sum of its parts. We're players and we are paid to perform, but we take our responsibilities to ourselves and to each other seriously. It also really helps, when the pressure is on, to feel that your teammates will have your back. The more experienced players can help the younger professionals to understand what it means to be a good professional and not to get too weighed down by mistakes and allow them to knock their confidence. Pressure comes from outside, of course, but also from the players themselves. Obviously, there is an expectation from the coaches, from your teammates, and the public as well to perform and to get results, but we have a good culture in Leinster and in Ireland that mistakes are fine as long as you're learning from them. The criticism is a hundred per cent constructive to make the player and the team better.

This came sharply into focus for me when we toured South Africa in 2024. We went out in the summer after a long and gruelling Six Nations and club season to play two test matches against pretty much the same side that had won the World Cup in 2023 – and that we had beaten in the pool stages of that tournament. Much has been made of the rivalry between the two teams, and there's always the 'best in the world' chat in the media, but I can remember Andy Farrell in the post-match press conference saying, 'I don't care. It's just two good sides and you wouldn't want to separate them… and you can join two or three, three or four countries into that.' He's right. The point of these rivalries is not to prove who is the best in the world: it's to push each team to come in and play the very best. Rivalry makes sport what it is.

In the first match, in Pretoria, we made a few mistakes early on to give the Springboks a couple of easy chances. When you're listening to the commentary, it's clear to see what those chances are, but on the field, in a fast-moving game, it's very different. We might have a game plan against a physical side like South Africa, but the opposition can throw something very different at you. A pass might not go to hand or they get the bounce of the ball, and the whole dynamic can change. The South Africans have a good lineout, a strong scrum and we were determined not to give them a foothold in the game that way, but we didn't always succeed. It was great to see Jamie Osborne score a try on his debut and we were unlucky that James Lowe's inspirational try wasn't allowed, but no excuses: we'd need to improve for the second test if we were to level the series.

The other thing that I won't forget about the match is our injury quota, which was pretty high. Apart from my dislocated little finger, which looked worse than it actually was, there was the much more significant issue of Dan Sheehan's ACL injury, which he sustained when tackling Eben Etzebeth, and Craig Casey's concussion after a tackle by RG Snyman, when his head bounced off the pitch. It was a really tough encounter and we were pretty battle-scarred afterwards. When two good sides meet, it's going to be full-on, and this truly was. What makes the difference, then? I think it comes down to digging in and showing your character as a unit. I can remember one of the pundits, I think it was Virgin Media's Matt Williams, saying, 'Champions get up when they can't.' That was our job in the second test in Durban.

Andy very much put it up to us in that week between the first and second tests and the result was the opposite of our first week's performance. 'It was a complete role reversal in the first half this week: I thought it was outstanding, as good as it gets.' The second half was, as our captain Caelan Doris said, 'a bit of a shitshow', and I gave away a penalty to South Africa, among a few, but Ciarán Frawley was an absolute hero. His two drop goals were unforgettable. I can't believe the way he settled himself to take the first one. And as for the second, 'It was immense how he had the courage to take it early,' said Andy Farrell. A game has so many variables that it's impossible to predict and sometimes hard for players to analyse afterwards, but in the second test, certainly in the first half, we stopped them playing their game and in the second half, we dug deep to hang on in there. That was a win, more than many, worth having.

The golfer Scottie Scheffler got a lot of attention at the 2025 British Open in Portrush when he talked about winning and questioned whether it really mattered that much.

> If I win, it's going to be awesome for two minutes, then
> we're going to get into next week and it's, 'Hey, you
> won two majors this year; how important is it to you
> to win the FedEx Cup playoffs?' It feels like you work
> your whole life to celebrate winning a tournament
> for, like, a few minutes, that kind of euphoric feeling.

I can see what he means, but to me it's not just about chasing that high. Sure, it's great, and sure there'll be another match the following week, but it's more about sharing the highs and the lows with the team. Maybe that's a difference between individual and team sports, but I think you have to enjoy the process as well as the outcome – and when the outcome is good, to really savour the moment. That's why I agree with Justin Rose's reply: 'The work and the journey to get there is the thrill. You want it to manifest into tournament wins and ticking off your goals and your dreams but really, the journey and the process of getting there is where you have to try to find the enjoyment.'

And when the outcome is bad, try not to dwell on it for too long. Losing is part of sport, part of life. I've done the sulking about it and there's no real reward to it. I can say that now after being in that place of feeling that it's all my fault, of making myself the victim in it, to a certain extent. I can confirm that there's no upside to this kind of thinking. It doesn't help you to move forward; it only keeps you stuck in a cycle of rumination and self-recrimination. The only way is to pick yourself up, dust yourself off and start again. What is it Samuel Beckett said? 'Try again. Fail again. Fail better.'

Win or lose, what gives me meaning in my job is sharing it with my teammates, my family and the fans and finding a way of enjoying the hard work of training, planning and preparation, and not just the elation of the wins. This brings me back to the quote from Marcus Aurelius at the beginning of this chapter, 'the obstacle is the way'. To me this means that losses are heartbreaking if you've put everything into the fight but they are also opportunities to get better, to work harder. If you just focus on the failure, nothing happens except recrimination. If you pick yourself up and say, 'Okay, what can I do better next week?' that's an entirely different conversation.

CHAPTER 10

CUTTING OUT THE NOISE

'It never ceases to amaze me: we all love ourselves more than other people, but care more about their opinion than our own.'

Marcus Aurelius, Meditations

The first time I watched Leinster play in Croke Park was in the semi-final of the Heineken Cup against Munster in 2009. I was thirteen and had gone with my cousin Sarah and I'll never forget it. The attendance was at the max, 82,000 supporters, a sea of blue and red: there truly is no better place than Croker on a match day, whether you're watching the finals of an All-Ireland or the historic England–Ireland match played in 2007.

I watched the then-Leinster coach Michael Cheika, my dad's hero, recalling the 2009 match recently, and feeling that it was an 'out of body' experience. He found it hard to understand how he'd emerged into the 'vortex of the cyclone' as he put it, as coach of the Leinster team and as an Australian. Leinster were very much the underdogs: Munster were an amazing team. That day Paul O'Connell was captaining a team that included Ronan O'Gara, Keith Earls, Peter Stringer... They had hammered Leinster in 2006, but for Leinster captain Brian O'Driscoll this year would be different.

> I believe it is going to be the biggest club game in world history so it will be nice to be part of. I know I won't be as stressed as I was for the semi-final in 2006 – that was probably the most nervous I have been for any game, it was horrible and I didn't enjoy it. I'm way more relaxed this week and treating it as another big, tough European game against undoubtedly the best team in Europe at the moment.

The result was a little piece of history, and I'll always remember O'Driscoll intercepting ROG's pass, bolting up the pitch for a try, with O'Gara desperately trying to catch him.

As Michael Cheika recalls, 'It's almost like we had no choice.' Leinster knew that pitting themselves against the best team in Europe was a great mark to aim for. Leinster won that match 25–6 and our renaissance began. Now, arguably, we are the dominant team in the country. We have a fantastic academy that really brings people through as young players and Leo Cullen has led us for the last ten years, in spite of all of the pressures. Recently, Jacques Nienaber has joined the coaching staff and he's an inspirational coach. According to commentator Bernard Jackman he's made us 'play like psychos'. I'm not sure what he means by that but we certainly defend aggressively.

Why have Leinster become such a force in this country? Well, there's been a lot of investment in the province. Perhaps it's the dominance of the rugby schools in Leinster – there's no denying that that's where most of the team comes from – and the province has close ties with the schools system. I can remember Stuart Lancaster used to coach schools' teams quite regularly when he was head coach of Leinster. The Sub Academy takes unformed players and gives them a chance, just like me. I came up through the academy system so I can attest that it's a world-class feeder for the senior team. Hugo Keenan, James Ryan, Max Deegan, and Jimmy O'Brien played with me in the Sub Academy and all progressed to play for their province. Leinster have their eye on players in school systems and keep the conveyer belt going, but players do come from the club system. Both Tadhg Furlong and Jamie Osborne came from rugby clubs. Some people argue that some players get overlooked in the club system, but it would have been impossible to ignore Tadhg. He was a brilliant Gaelic football player: there is footage of him playing as a teenager, wiping out the opposition in a club game. It's probably fortuitous that he chose rugby!

There's also no arguing with the fact that the Leinster area now contains almost half the country's population, and that's a big pool of potential. I also think there's something in the argument that our system can guarantee more good players than can the club system in the UK. We're spotted earlier and brought into the system as teenagers. In Leinster, the team can change week on week and I think that's a luxury for us, because we have so many players in the building. We used 58 different players this year, trying out different combinations to see what clicked, as well as giving younger players match experience.

But then something that Jamie Heaslip said a while back caught my attention. He was talking about the French, who are playing fantastically at club level: 'They have more players, more clubs, more entry points into the game, and if you don't make it in one club, you can kind of bounce around numerous clubs to find your spot. Whereas in Ireland, there's four professional clubs.' He has a point. We can't overcome our size as a country, but we can boost all four provinces. And we can spread the net a little wider when it comes to finding new talent. Bernard Jackman pointed to Bordeaux Bègles flanker Mahamadou Diaby as an example. Born in a deprived area of Paris, Diaby was initially a kickboxer before deciding that he had what it took to be a rugby player. Racing 92 gave him a trial on the basis that he asked for one, and when they discovered his talent, they invested in his potential. This is the kind of grassroots recruiting that the GAA does so well. It'd be great to see it in rugby too. The more people we have playing this game, the better.

Leinster won the Champions Cup in 2018. Since then, we've been so close, but have yet to claim the trophy again. Why? When I was asked about this, I made a remark that will come back to haunt me: 'You don't see many URC or Pro14s or whatever you have on the jersey. You see those Champion Cup stars on the jersey.' We went on to win the URC in 2025 and were ecstatic about it, but when you haven't won the most coveted prize in a while, I suppose you can get a bit fixated on it.

Our loss to Northampton Saints in the 2025 season semi-final of the Champions Cup really hurt. All losses do, but this one was even more brutal. There's a lot of expectation around a team like Leinster, that we'll just blow other clubs out of the water. That's disrespectful to other clubs for a start, and Northampton have some brilliant players: Fin Smith, Fraser Dingwall, Henry Pollock, Alex Mitchell, to name a few, and they're a tight unit.

All that week, the chatter was that we'd beat them by 30 points, but there was no way we'd be that complacent. It was a terrific game of rugby between two well-matched sides and Northampton's attack was relentless. They just kept on coming. We managed to push them hard in the second half, but we made a few mistakes. I had a penalty awarded against me in a scrum, which wasn't ideal. Northampton really brought it to us and we just didn't have quite enough in reply. Leo was right in saying that we hadn't been accurate enough towards the end, and as he said, 'this is one that's going to sting for a long time'. It did – their game plan worked, and as Leo said, 'when we fall behind, we get a bit jittery.' I think that's fair.

I don't think we were really prepared for the outcry afterwards, though, both from former professionals and from the public. If we hadn't got past the knockout rounds of the competition, the response would be understand-able; but we were getting to the semis and up there with the best teams. I think that expectations are high around a team like Leinster, and there can be a feeling that we're almost entitled to a championship, but none of us on the team thinks like that. Perhaps it's projected onto us, but it's not something we feel.

Playing in the URC feels special because it involves so many more players from the team and so many of us had gone through losses in the past few years. In the end, it felt amazing to win the URC and, more so, to win in Croke Park, but there was also a sense of relief that we had something to show for our efforts. We did it and we did it well. I think the dark days of losses make the wins all the better. Maybe you have to go through those dark days to appreciate the good ones. I should know that better than most.

'Keep the abuse coming. We don't mind. Thick skins.' Leo Cullen said after our loss to Northampton, and he was right. The thing is, I'd say that we used the 'abuse' to fuel our final two performances against Glasgow and the Bulls in the URC. We really gave it our all. In the end we won the URC, and I can confirm that it felt great, as the pictures of me wearing goggles and spraying the changing room with champagne will attest. But we weren't complacent then either. As Leo explained before the match:

Glasgow won't be afraid, you saw them last weekend against the Stormers [winning 36–18]. They have that slogan, 'Whatever It Takes', so they certainly push the boundaries. They are the reigning champions, they won away last year in Limerick in a semi, and went away to win a final. We know they'll be hard to handle, tough to play against. They're very, very competitive in all facets of the game.

They were, and the final scoreline of 37–19 belied a tough game.

It's a tough position to be in, where you get so far but don't make it any further – maybe there's a psychological aspect to that – but days like that definitely add to our resilience, because we have to dig deep then and find a response in spite of all the commentary. We can't just down tools and give up – we have to push on and try to achieve more. Besides, you can't be a winner all the time. If you only think in terms of winning, you'll operate from a place of fear that you'll lose and that's not the right mindset. You need to accept losses and move on. Otherwise, you can't play freely. I learned the hard way that ruminating over losses is not going to help; learning from them and moving on to the next game is.

We have terrific fans at Leinster, but people love to sit on the couch and analyse the game. Fair enough – that's part of the fun of being a fan. They have a ringside seat and can see things more clearly than we can down on the pitch. We're playing in real time, in the moment, and there are so many variables that happen all at once. We also make mistakes, and while we try to correct them, we need to move on quickly. A game is in constant motion, constantly evolving and we don't have the luxury of standing back and thinking before we play. With the benefit of replays, the viewers can see what should and shouldn't have happened, but we're in the thick of it, responding to the other team in the moment. That's all we can do. I don't resent the fans for being fans, taking the team to task and analysing the plays. Of course we prepare for matches: we have our team meetings; we review the other team's plays on video to break down what they're doing and how they're approaching the game. We come up with scenarios and strategies and we practise them, but what happens on the ground can change that in a heartbeat. You can only do so much preparation. What matters is what happens when you come out of the tunnel and onto the pitch.

Nowadays, everyone is a critic. There are the pundits, who have a lot of expertise and who fill the half-time slot with observations and consider the game at the end, all of which is entirely fair. We don't exist in a vacuum and sometimes the criticism is valid. It can even spur us on to improve. However, with the rise of social media, there are also thousands of people giving their opinion on matches who may never have played a game in their lives. There's nothing wrong with this, of course, but as elite athletes we know just how much has gone into our training, preparation and so on. We don't just rock up to play on the day.

But as players, we just can't get sucked into it: there's

too much of it and it really doesn't help. And it can get nasty. When Antoine Dupont was injured during our Six Nations clash with France, Tadhg Beirne and myself came in for some terrible abuse on social media. I can't speak for Tadhg, except to say that he's a fantastic player and a complete gent, who would absolutely not injure someone intentionally. Neither would I. That's not the kind of player either of us is. There was no malicious intent from either of us and seeing a player go off injured is always tough.

When I was a younger player, I used to read all the match reports and absorb all the feedback, using it as a stick to beat myself with, but now I know better. I can't let the opinion of a pundit, no matter how experienced, or the emotional opinions of a fan who feels short-changed sway me – otherwise I'd never set foot on the pitch! I used to look for validation in match reports, taking the opinions of pundits and fans to heart. I used to search for my name on X or Instagram and see what people were saying about me. At the time, it almost motivated me: *I'll show these guys*, I'd think angrily, but over the years I've learned to block that because there are plenty of people in my life whose opinion matters more to me. My family, my friends, my teammates. But when France's head coach complained about the Dupont incident, some French fans turned their attention to Elaine. Threatening messages poured in, full of abusive comments and general malice, and that made me so angry. I remember reading Andrew Conway's column and agreeing with him when he said, 'It's enormously sad that people who are probably respectable enough in formal life, go on the internet and send direct messages based on something that happened in a game.'

Social media has really changed the nature of the criticism we receive – for better and for worse. Where once they might have shouted at the TV, now, when someone wants to criticise you, they have a platform to do it on. People can post whatever they like, or hide behind fake social media accounts. These people only see the players when they're playing, when they're out there on the field, but we're more than just rugby players. We're brothers, husbands, boyfriends, sons – there's so much more to the players than what you see for eighty minutes on a Saturday.

Social media can create a distorted reality, and it's a tough place to be in. I've tried to shut myself off from it – there's nothing worse than seeing something written about you after a tough game. It doesn't bother me any more, but I hate to see it bothering the people I love. Elaine left social media for a while after the French game, when she got some nasty messages about our unborn son. I also remember that following the New Zealand game in the World Cup someone messaged her to suggest that she divorce me. Thankfully she hasn't decided to act on that yet!

I'm not sure I'll ever get used to being a public persona or to the spotlight that can sometimes be shone on us as individuals and even on our partners and families. I think this is the reality of the modern game. While I'm always happy to stop for a selfie, and most fans only want to have a chat or get me to sign a jersey, sometimes fans can get a bit carried away. I have been approached by people, often with a few drinks taken, with their opinions on the game and my performance in it. All I can say is that I know the work I've done and what it's like to be a professional and while everyone is entitled to their opinion, it's good to remember that I'm a person, just like them.

Here's where Marcus Aurelius comes in handy.

> If an action or utterance is appropriate then it's appropriate for you. Don't be put off by other people's comments and criticism. If it's right to say or do it, then it's the right thing for you to do or say. The others obey their own lead, follow their own impulses. Don't be distracted. Keep walking. Follow your own nature and follow Nature – along the road they share.

It's easier said than done, I know, but I think it's really important to let people have their views and to respect that but also not to be afraid to hold your own position and to follow your own path. If you allow people's opinions to shape your behaviour, you won't be able to be fully yourself or able to live your own life. You'll always be chasing validation and approval from outside yourself. Take it from me, it doesn't work.

CHAPTER 11

NO GREATER HONOUR

'Nothing is more difficult and therefore more precious, than to be able to decide.'

Napoleon Bonaparte

It's July 2025 and at this point in the Lions tour of Australia, the hotel room has changed. We have a view of Sydney Harbour, and that's amazing. I can see all the sailing boats and the iconic Opera House against the blue sky. It's idyllic. However, I much prefer looking at our newly installed video doorbell in Dublin and seeing Elaine and our son waving to me. 'Say hello to Daddy!' Elaine is saying, waving the baby's little hand.

Max is now six weeks old and the fact that he's in Ireland and I'm twelve thousand miles away seems surreal. I know that I'll never be on tour with the Lions in Australia again, but I also know that I won't be a new dad again and missing out on these weeks is really tough. It's hard to explain the mixture of guilt and excitement I'm feeling on this tour. I desperately wanted to be here, especially as

I missed out in 2021, but at the same time, I'm thinking I really miss Elaine and Max.

Looking back, it's odd to think how cut and dried I was about things before Max arrived. Going on the Lions tour was the be-all and end-all of my career, the once-in-a- lifetime thing that I might not do again. I was blinded to the fact that having my first child is never going to happen again either. As soon as he was born though, I can remember thinking to myself, *This is what I've always wanted. To be a dad.* I have no idea what kind of dad I'll be: I can't imagine I'll be a stern taskmaster – in fact, I suspect I'll be a bit of a pushover – but if I'm half as good as my own dad, I'll be happy.

I've often thought about what fatherhood is like for us modern dads. In my dad's time, the rules were simpler. I don't think dads did much of the nappy changing or feeding or playing with the baby. I don't have my own mum to ask what kind of a dad Ernie was in the early days, but I know how much of a role model he was later on. He was a traditional dad in that he left the house every morning to go to work; and yet he was also ahead of his time in being there as a support to me and my sisters when he was grieving himself. He was the one who gave us lifts and helped us with our homework, filling Mum's roles as well as his own. Maybe that's why I've always wanted to be a dad. Even in the years when I didn't get on with him so well, I always looked up to him and the way he got through Mum's death and raising us three. So, when Elaine came along, I knew that I wanted to create a family with her. When you find that right person, it comes naturally, I think. And Dad was the kind of role model I wanted to emulate.

I met Elaine in the twenty-first-century way, on a dating app. I had no clue how to talk to women, so presenting myself on an app made sense. We matched quite early on, but I'm sure I said something stupid when I messaged her at first, because it didn't go any further for a bit. We did follow each other on Instagram, though. In the meantime, I can remember going to my first ever Leinster Rugby ball and being so stricken with nerves that I had a bit too much to drink beforehand. Little did I know, Elaine was working at the event that night, so I can't imagine what kind of impression I made on her. All she said about it was 'Did you enjoy yourself at the ball?' I didn't detect any sarcasm in her question. I'm glad to say that she's come with me to many Leinster balls since, so she's forgiven me.

I plucked up the courage to ask her out and I can still remember standing on Grafton Street waiting to meet her after work, hoping that she wouldn't stand me up. She didn't, and a 'quick drink' turned into a pub crawl until six in the morning. I knew that we had clicked, because we didn't stop talking and laughing all night. Because Elaine is from Bray, I ordered her a taxi from town and escorted her home, which is, she tells me, when she knew I was a keeper. The fact that we both fell asleep in the taxi showed just what a great time we'd had.

I knew immediately that she was the one for me: Elaine is funny, full of life and great fun to be with, but really strong and grounded as well. She's also endlessly supportive and the minute I share my day with her, good or bad, I relax. I know that when I'm with her, I'm sharing everything fifty-fifty. She's my partner in every way.

Proposing to Elaine after we'd been together for a few years was a no-brainer. I knew that this was the woman I wanted to spend the rest of my life with. The ultimate test was buying a dog together, and that's how Pablo came into our lives. I can't remember whose idea it was to buy an Old English bulldog, but he looked incredibly cute as a puppy. We brought him home to meet Cheika, who didn't completely hate him. Pablo was definitely a dog who resembled his owner, a big slobbering goofball who became my right-hand man. He took a starring role in the Netflix documentary and was a great man for chasing a ball. I would often take him to the rugby pitches near the house and puck a sliotar for him to wear him out.

He could destroy any ball or toy and we had to ensure any toys were indestructible.

However, when I went away on the Ireland tour of New Zealand in 2022, he acted up for Elaine no end. One evening, Elaine had invited her family over for dinner and Pablo disappeared into the garden. There was a bit of shuffling in the hedge and then Pablo came in, a distressed look on his face and a six-inch piece of bamboo sticking out of his rear end. He proceeded to make a huge mess all over the house and Elaine and her family had to put plastic sheets down in the car before taking him to the UCD Veterinary Hospital where he had to be put under to remove the stick. He came back happy the next day, but he'd destroyed the floor in our kitchen. It was never the same afterwards. I don't think Elaine's family was either.

Pablo looked a bit frightening but he was the neediest dog ever. Elaine and I had a rule that he wasn't to get up on the couch, but the minute we sat down, he'd jump up on top of us, much to Dad's alarm. Dad is not a dog person: he's used to working dogs on the farm and has no time for a spoiled couch doggy, but when we were expecting Max, it was decided that Pablo might be better rooming with Dad for a bit. I wondered what Pablo would make of Dad's tough love, but one time I came over to the house to visit, and through the living room window I could see the two of them sitting together on the couch. When I came in, Dad jumped up and pretended to give out to him: 'What are you doing on the couch?' I wasn't fooled. The two of them are inseparable now and I think Elaine feels a bit more relaxed without the canine chaos.

I proposed on holiday in Nice after the 2022 tour of New Zealand. I had it all planned out beforehand. I had the ring and I knew that I wanted to propose at the viewing point on Castle Hill that overlooks the Promenade des Anglais. The view of the Mediterranean would be perfect, I thought, and it was a nice quiet spot. I am not a fan of public proposals.

The problem was that the weather was incredibly hot and as we climbed the steps up to the viewing point, Elaine began to get tired. 'I can't go any further,' she said eventually. 'I think I need some air conditioning.' *We're only halfway up*, I thought. *I can't propose here.* I'd have to think of a Plan B, I realised as I helped her down the steps and back along the promenade, which was jam-packed with tourists and locals. For a few days afterwards, I looked for suitable places, so afraid of leaving the ring behind somewhere that I put it in my backpack and carried it around with me everywhere. Eventually, my moment came in a lovely restaurant by the harbour. After dinner, as we sipped a glass of wine, I waited for Elaine to turn to look at the boats in the harbour and when she did, I quickly got down on bended knee. I called her name and when she turned around, I asked her to marry me. It was perfect. She said yes, thankfully. Then we went to an Irish pub to celebrate! There, over a bottle of champagne, we toasted our future and listened to a great band called Stolen City, who we ended up asking to play at our wedding.

In my profession, trying to organise a wedding isn't easy. We have no idea of our schedule until the week beforehand and the off season is so short nowadays that it's hard to plan. Thankfully, Elaine was much better at that than me. We picked the only free week I had before the 2023 World Cup and selected the date, 6 July, and the venue, the Glasson Lakehouse, which overlooks Lough Ree. It's a really relaxed place with fantastic views, so it was perfect for the family event we had planned – which ended up being about two hundred people. We had to fit in our wedding around three or four of the other lads on the team who were also getting married, but it didn't make it any less special to us. Elaine had seven bridesmaids, including her sister, Niamh, and I had four groomsmen, my four oldest friends – Josh Percival, Josh Murphy, Andrew Meates and Chris Wallace – so there was a real entourage.

Elaine knew that I'd be missing Mum on my wedding day, so she had a little pin made for me with Mum's photo on it to wear inside my jacket, which was incredibly thoughtful. I treasure that pin and keep it close, bringing it with me on every away trip since.

I was a bundle of nerves until I saw Elaine walk up the aisle towards me in her beautiful dress and I relaxed instantly. When you know, you know, and I definitely knew. We had such a fun family day, full of good speeches and laughter. Dad surprised us by making an emotional speech, talking about how much Mum and now Elaine meant to him, and it brought tears to my eyes. Dad is a shy man and not given to making speeches, so the fact that he stood up in front of everyone made it extra special. It was great to be able to truly enjoy my own wedding day, to dance and to laugh, and in the end to be able to walk off into the sunset with my best friend, now my wife.

Fast forward two years and we're parents. Taking Max home after the hospital was amazing and terrifying at the same time. It was a bit of a rollercoaster. You get home with a tiny baby and you think, *Why on earth would the hospital let us leave with a baby?* It was hard to believe that we were in charge of this ship now: there were no helpful midwives to take him or anyone to tell us what was going on when he was doing something we hadn't googled. But when I stripped the anxiety away, I kept telling myself, *Okay, we were made to do this. That's our job as humans.*

We've got this. Not always easy in the middle of the night when he's crying and we're not sure why, but in my heart, I know that it's everything we ever wanted.

As a problem-solver, I was all over Instagram before the birth, looking up tutorials on baby swaddling and practising on a pillow and with towels while I was in the Irish camp in Carton House. When I first showed her my swaddling expertise, Elaine was impressed. 'Where did you learn that?' Fail to prepare, prepare to fail! But it definitely made me feel better about the unknown, being able to prepare for it in a practical way. It's an elite athlete's instinct to prepare as much as possible, to remove any element of guesswork from the equation – it's something we do every single day. But having a baby is not like training for a match, so I had to accept that there was only so much I could do.

Learning the ropes gave me something to do, though: Elaine was the champion throughout pregnancy and childbirth. I'm completely in awe of her – but, as the man, you know it's not really about you. Even when you're in the hospital, in the room, you feel as if you're in the way, but after the baby is born, you can actually be useful.

I fell in love with Max the moment I saw him. Some dads have told me that they didn't feel a connection to the baby at first and it wasn't until they got a bit older and began to make eye contact or babble that that connection happened.

In my case, I felt the link between us immediately. Babies don't make eye contact at this stage, but when I spoke, he would settle, as if he recognised my voice. Something about that connection gave me a boost of confidence, so even though I was nervous, I knew that I could figure out what to do. I felt confident that I could take over when Elaine needed it, so in the first couple of weeks I made myself useful by taking the night shifts so that she could recover. There's a benefit to being an insomniac, and I had just discovered what it is.

Having Max is everything we ever wanted. We are so lucky that he's completely healthy and thriving. Considering what Elaine went through before his birth, with two miscarriages in 2024 and the sense of anxiety and doubt she felt this time, it's all the sweeter. Elaine would often tell me that, because this was her third pregnancy, she couldn't be completely happy until our son was born; she found it hard to truly celebrate until she saw him. The only thing I could really do was listen. Men are great for being solution-focused, but I knew that Elaine just wanted to be heard and validated, rather than me 'fixing' things for her. Her worries about the pregnancy were completely normal because of what she'd been through in losing the first two pregnancies.

When we first learned that we were expecting Max, there were so many conflicting emotions: joy, relief, worry, uncertainty, hope. All of that stuff. Elaine's mum is still around, and I couldn't help wondering what my mum would have said and done to help. I know that she would have been brilliant, and it was hard not to feel her absence.

We were on holiday last summer when Elaine decided to post about our experience on Instagram. It wasn't something she'd planned, but comments by US Vice President JD Vance on pregnancy rights spurred her to share her story. Elaine felt compelled to speak out about her own experience of losing two pregnancies because she felt so strongly about his remarks: 'sharing that I've had a miscarriage is absolutely never something I thought I'd share on my Instagram but I thought it was so important to speak out against small-minded men who think they have a say on women's bodies and choices.'

I felt so proud of Elaine for speaking out. Her comments obviously resonated with a lot of people. We hadn't realised how common miscarriage is until we were inundated with messages of support and people sharing their stories. Miscarriage is something that people don't really talk about much and Elaine was really buoyed up by the support of other women who'd gone through it. I was so proud of her and did everything I could to support her.

As a man, I felt that I almost didn't deserve to feel it as strongly because I hadn't gone through it myself – until I looked through all the messages I'd had from men about their experience of miscarriages. So many of them told me that they'd struggled for years with fertility issues, or that they'd had a miscarriage, or two, or more, and gone on to have a healthy baby. Sharing my story helped them to understand that they weren't the only ones going through it. It really helped me to know that I wasn't alone either. I suppose when any kind of adversity happens, you feel that it's only affecting you or that you're the only one going through it, but the guys' messages made me feel so much better. Sharing is such an empowering thing. I think that's the main thing that I've tried to do when I'm talking about mental health or any kind of adversity – to open the door for other people and let them know that they're not the only people going through it. What's been an amazing bonus is that I've got a lot out of that too.

Last year, 2024, was a particularly tough year because I was absent quite a lot. There was the tour of South Africa and the pressures of the Six Nations to deal with and I know that Elaine felt it. As a player, it's really hard to park what's going on in your life and go out and perform, but you have to, even for just that eighty minutes on the pitch. I owed it to Elaine, who'd gone through so much, and all the people who'd been in touch to support us and to share their stories.

CHAPTER 12

THE THINGS WE DO FOR LOVE

'When you arise in the morning, think of what a precious privilege it is to be alive – to breathe, to think, to enjoy, to love.'

Marcus Aurelius, Meditations

We went into the final round of the 2024 Six Nations facing Scotland, knowing a win would seal the championship. We'd lost to England the week before in a heated battle that had ended with them easing ahead 23–22. We were pretty humbled by that loss, particularly as it had cost us the Grand Slam. For our last match, we knew that a very important person might be leaving us: there were rumours that our captain Peter O'Mahony might retire after this season. Also, Scotland had been dangerous all tournament and we weren't taking anything for granted. The Aviva was packed and the nerves were real. We started well. Bundee and James Lowe made big carries early and we built pressure. Dan Sheehan scored a try and I remember a scrum just inside their 22 where we got a penalty. Jack Crowley slotted it and we settled.

Scotland came back though, attacking relentlessly. Finn Russell kicked two penalties to take us to 7–6.

At half-time we regrouped. Faz told us to trust our shape and to wear the Scottish defence down. In the second half we turned the screw. I carried off a maul and we built phases, and a scrum penalty ensured a big territory gain. We kept the foot down, but missed three tries that might have been – from Tadhg Furlong, Garry Ringrose and Robbie Henshaw. When Ewan Ashman was sent to the sin bin, we saw our chance. Ronan Kelleher flicked the ball to me five metres out and I pushed for the line. Face-in-the-mud time again, but it was a try. The match ended at 17-13 in our favour. We celebrated in the dressing room with the trophy and a few beers. It wasn't flashy but it had been earned. That campaign showed our depth and our grit. We'd grown again. I had grown.

I'd need that grit to support Elaine through the next year. When we learned about this pregnancy late in 2024, we were ecstatic, but at the same time bracing for impact. We'd go from scan to scan, each one reassuring us, but leaving us in limbo until the next one. We were fortunate in that we could afford to go for a couple of private scans for reassurance and that really made a difference. We could say, 'Great, he was thriving at the last scan and he's thriving now,' so that took some of the anxiety away. We had a bit more peace of mind and clarity. We didn't have to think *what if?* We could focus on making plans for the early weeks of his life.

Naming him was actually quite straightforward after all of the other complications. We used an app called Kinder, in which you put in all your interests and ideas and it comes up with a list of possibilities. Now, in fairness, we did have some clangers: my interest in Norse mythology led to a lot of Thors and Odins! But we both knew that Max was the one. That's probably a good thing because I remember coming home one day from training and Elaine said, 'Oh, I had something delivered today,' proudly showing me a nappy bag with his name stitched across the front. *Okay,* I thought, *I guess that's his name* ... But Elaine and I made a joint decision not to name him publicly until we were ready. We didn't want him on any social media posts or in gossip magazines or anything like that before we shared the name news with our families. Max is his own man, his name is his own and he won't be part of our public lives, but like every new parent, I'm dying to show him off. I love looking at the photos Elaine sends me to see how he's changing, bouncing gently in his cradle, taking everything in from his perch on the sofa.

And yet the irony isn't lost on me that this once-in-a-lifetime experience has happened at exactly the same time as my first Lions tour. I won't be there for Elaine and Max and I'll never have those weeks of his life again. So many people have said to me that because he's so young, the baby won't miss me because he doesn't even recognise me. I know they're trying to make me feel better, but that's not the point. I'll miss his first smile, the first time he turns his head when he hears my voice; I'll even miss the night shifts and sitting with him in the darkness as he snuffles away on my shoulder. And I'll miss Elaine and being able to be half-useful to her, even though we've both put lots of supports in place. Elaine's mum and dad, Sean and Therese, are going to be there and we have help coming during the day for a few hours to do a bit of housework so it doesn't all pile up while Elaine is doing the important stuff. We are aware of just what a privilege that is. And yet, I also know how much of a privilege it is to be playing for the Lions. A friend asked me if the thought of staying at home had entered my mind. Of course it had, but at the same time I knew that this chance might not come along again.

When I lost out in 2021, I was determined that it wouldn't happen again. I set a reminder on my phone for July 2025 and my morning alarms came with a message:

Get out of bed. You won't make the Lions by sleeping in. Four years of preparing, of early mornings and tough matches. Could I give it all up?

Before he was born, I remember telling Elaine, 'I need to do this after I missed out the last time.' Elaine was apprehensive not just about the pregnancy but about being alone with a newborn when she was still recovering. She was anxious about me going to the other side of the world. Ironically, when Max was born our feelings switched. I looked at him and thought, *How on earth will I be able to leave you?* Elaine, on the other hand, felt such a huge sense of relief when he arrived safe and sound that she knew that with the right help, she could do it. She said, 'You need to go and I need to stay. We both need to do this. It'll be the best thing for both of us.'

It's amazing how much your life can shift in 24 hours. We professional athletes are self-centred by nature. We have to be to do what we need to do: all those weekend matches, the events and the training, the unpredictable schedule are part of our lives, but they can be difficult for our partners and families and, even though it's not for ever, it's not easy for those around us. But when my son arrived, I had a complete 180-degree shift in perspective. *This is the important thing,* I thought. *This is what really matters.* You think you have a clear hierarchy of what's important in life, then you attend the birth of your child and you go, *Oh, everything's changed.*

Finally, both Elaine and I are in a good place about the Lions and about the early months of Max's life. I look forward to being there for the next eighteen years. And if by some miracle I make another Lions tour, well, we'll cross that bridge when we come to it.

It's now a dull and chilly Saturday in Melbourne and my throat is hoarse from singing. We've been through 'Sweet Caroline' and 'Dirty Old Town' (we had to teach our Welsh, English and Scottish teammates that song) and the celebrations are about to begin. We've won the second test with a last-second try from Hugo Keenan and we're ecstatic. There really is nothing like coming out in front of 90,000 people in Melbourne's Cricket Ground to get the blood pumping.

Our first test match was at the Suncorp Stadium in Brisbane and we ran onto the pitch to the tune of AC/DC's 'Hell's Bells'. Tadhg Beirne won a jackal penalty at the first breakdown and Finn Russell converted it before scoring our first try seven minutes later. Max Jorgensen got one back for the Aussies at the 29th minute, but Tom Curry dived over for our second try to give us a 17-5 lead at half time. Our attacks and defence had been strong and we had them under pressure. Dan

Sheehan scored another try in the corner before I came on for Genge at 49 minutes, and while our hosts had a try by Joseph-Aukuso Suaalii disallowed in the 60th minute it took until the 68th minute for them to put together 10 phases close to the line, with Carlo Tizzano getting the touchdown. Another penalty for us, and a consolation try by Tate McDermott for the Wallabies, and it's all over. We've passed our first test with a score of 27-19. Faz's plans had worked, we had dominated physically, really pushing the Wallabies and making them work.

It had been a bit scrappy though. Maro Itoje, who's been an inspirational leader, said afterwards that we could have done better, and he had a point. The scrums didn't all go our way, which says as much about Joe Schmidt's leadership of the Wallabies as it does about our efforts.

That first test was pretty much the first time our feet touched the ground after criss-crossing the country playing two matches a week. The tour had started with great fanfare in Perth, when we played Western Force at the Optus Stadium. I came off the bench after fifty minutes and I knew my job was simple: bring energy, bring power and keep the standard high. We'd built a strong lead by the time I got on, but there's no such thing as a quiet shift – every carry, every scrum, every ruck matters. Western Force had been stubborn early on, but our lads had broken them open with pace and precision. The Force had made us work, especially at the breakdown, where we lost a few too many turnovers for comfort. Tomos Williams was electric before his injury – his tempo set the tone. Elliot Daly and Garry Ringrose were clinical and our maul was doing serious damage. Watching it unfold from the sideline, I was itching to get involved.

When I came on, I focused on locking down the scrum and adding some bite around the fringes. We kept the pressure on and the scoreboard kept ticking. I had one carry where I managed to punch through a couple of defenders and get us quick ball – it's those little moments that help keep the momentum alive. The atmosphere in Optus was deadly – big crowd, big noise and a real sense that the tour had properly begun. We ran in eight tries and while I didn't cross the line myself, it felt good to be part of a pack that had laid the foundation for such a dominant win. After the final whistle, there was a buzz in the dressing room. We'd made a statement – not just in the scoreline, but in how we played. Ruthless, connected and hungry.

In the second match in Brisbane against the Queensland Reds, the place was a furnace. The kind of heat that hits you in the lungs before the first whistle. But once we were out there, under the lights at Suncorp, it was all business. The Reds had talked up their physicality all week and we were ready to meet it head-on. From the first scrum, I knew we had them. We got a solid hit and I could feel their tighthead shifting under pressure. That's the kind of moment that sets the tone. We were sharp across the park – Tommy Freeman was electric and Duhan van der Merwe was a wrecking ball.

My try came just before the half-hour mark. We were camped on their line after a series of carries and I spotted a seam off the ruck. I dropped the shoulder and drove through. It wasn't pretty – most of what I do is never pretty – but it was over the line and that's what counts. I came off around the fifty-minute mark, job mostly done. We were in control by then and the bench brought fresh energy to finish the job. Maro was immense, Jac Morgan was everywhere and Finn kept the tempo high. We ran in seven tries in total and the 52–12 scoreline reflected our dominance.

Sydney marked a change in temperature both literally and on the pitch. We were playing New South Wales's Waratahs in the Allianz Stadium and the weather was a lot cooler. It was one of those nights where we were grateful for the win – but we knew it could've been a lot cleaner. The Waratahs brought real bite and we never quite shook them off. Watching it unfold on the bench, I could feel the tension in every breakdown, every knock-on, every missed chance.

We started well enough – Huw Jones finished a sharp move early and when he added a second just after the half-hour, it looked like we might pull away. But the Tahs wouldn't go quietly. Their defence was gritty and they kept turning us over at key moments. We were pinged repeatedly at the breakdown and it felt like every time we built pressure, we let them off the hook. The second half was more of the same: stop-start, scrappy and frustrating. Alex Mitchell's try gave us some breathing space, but we couldn't land the knockout blow. We had chances late on – multiple lineouts in the corner, a disallowed try for obstruction and even a final surge after the 80-minute mark – but nothing stuck. Duhan getting bundled into touch in the dying seconds summed it up. The final scoreline said it all: 10–21. A tough victory, hard won. It's never easy sitting one out, but it gives you a different lens – you can see the game in full: the flow, the pressure, the missed chances.

When we arrived in the country's capital, Canberra, to play our match against ACT Brumbies in the GIO Stadium, I started on the sideline, feeling the cool air, enjoying the packed crowd and in the Brumbies a team that had definitely come to play.

We started scrappily. Blair Kinghorn took a knock early and before we'd settled, the Brumbies were over for the first try. They were physical, direct and clever around the fringes.

We hit back through Ollie Chessum after a monster scrum and Lowe's finish was pure Lions rugby – fluid, fast and clinical. But we couldn't shake them. Every time we looked like pulling away, they found a way back in. Corey Toole's try exposed us out wide and Hudson Creighton's score off a five-metre scrum was a gut punch. We dominated territory, but we let them hang around. Three disallowed tries didn't help and we had to settle for a penalty when we should've had more.

Still, there were bright spots. Ringrose's dummy and finish was class, Marcus Smith looked sharp and van der Flier's maul try was textbook. Finn kept the scoreboard ticking and Maro led with real presence. We won, but we leaked four tries and that's not the standard we're chasing. It was clear: we were building something strong, but we still had a way to go. We knew that the test matches would be tight and that we'd need to be more ruthless, more accurate and more connected.

A lot happened between the first and the second test. The Wallabies' two key players, Rob Valetini and Will Skelton, returned to the squad. I swapped places with Ellis Genge, and Garry Ringrose withdrew from selection following a concussion sustained in the Brumbies match. There are now protocols around concussion and they are strictly observed.

Thankfully, there's a much greater awareness of player welfare nowadays. Games aren't quite as brutal as they were even ten or fifteen years ago. As a kid, I remember watching the Lions play in 2009, and in one game against South Africa, Brian O'Driscoll took two big head-on-head hits and still stayed on the pitch. Ronan O'Gara later admitted to the *Irish Times* that he was knocked out on the pitch at one stage in that same game, but he stumbled back to his feet and kept going. He got a huge gash above his left eye, but it was bandaged up and he played on. That would never happen now.

We've come a long way from the days when admitting to being injured was seen as a sign of weakness. This was made clear when Garry had the courage to tell the Lions coaches that he was experiencing some symptoms of concussion during training, ruling himself out of the second test match. It was incredibly selfless to do that, and while it was gutting for Garry, putting himself out of contention for the match just goes to show his character. I think it was an extremely hard thing to do, especially given the magnitude of the game, but it's a testament to the player and person he is that he put the team first and handed over to Huw Jones.

The second test was an absolute cracker, a rollercoaster from start to finish. They really had us rattled in the early stages of the first half. The energy and dominance of the Wallabies, with Valetini and Skelton back from injury, was phenomenal, particularly in the first twenty minutes, and it took us a while to find an answer. We lost a total of 39 tackles, and two penalties, with Tommy Freeman heading to the sin bin. Trailing 23–5 by the middle of the first half, we had to dig deep and find a way of responding to the Wallabies. The important thing in these situations is not to panic and lose the head. We kept calm. Jack Conan and Jamison Gibson-Park set up Tom Curry for a try and Finn Russell's massive kick to touch allowed Huw Jones to nudge the ball over the line. We went into half-time with the nerves settled, and after a pep talk from Maro and from Ellis, we came out for the second half resolute and, most important, calm. The Wallabies had burned off their early energy and we took advantage of that. I came off for Ellis, and James Ryan and Jac Morgan came on, giving us the energy we needed to push hard. James Lowe passed to Tadhg Beirne for our third try. In the 79th minute, we were within two points of the Wallabies – in the 80th we'd won, thanks to a try from Hugo Keenan that will go down in the history books.

The wait to see if the try would stand was agonising. Jac got incredibly low to clear the ball out and I can't see what else he could have done. Carlo Tizzano went back on his heels, but there was no foul play. Thankfully, the referee agreed. When Hugo put the ball over the line, I was standing by the edge of the pitch, the crowd roaring. Hugo had really been through it in this tour, suffering from a nasty bug that kept him out for twelve days, so to play like that and score the defining try of the game in the very last minute is a testament to the man's perseverance.

So far, this tour has been an incredible experience, everything I could have wished for. The friendships that I've formed here, the messing, the craic, but also the sheer hard work that's gone into each and every match has been fantastic. Getting to know the guys from the other countries has been a revelation: I know it's been said, but we've really bonded as a unit, in my case with my fellow props. I've loved sitting round and shooting the breeze with Ellis, Pierre Schoeman, Will Stuart and Finlay Bealham. Pierre's sense of humour is second to none. I'm not sure that I love us props being described as 'like bison, herding together', but it's probably true. I prefer Pierre's description of us as gladiators. We all love our Norse mythology and our steaks! We also work as a team; when Ellis was selected for the first test, Pierre and I were the first to congratulate him, and when I was selected for the second, Ellis was first up to shake my hand. We've shared the loosehead burdens and formed a lifelong bond. Ellis has also been on hand for some much-needed baby advice.

Max is now nine weeks old, and when I get back to Ireland, he'll be almost eleven weeks. In every photo Elaine sends me, he looks different. He's gone from fitting nicely into the crook of my elbow, his head resting on my arm, to sitting in his cradle, waving his hands and kicking for Ireland. It's been a huge sacrifice for Elaine. She's had help from Sean and Therese, her mum and dad, who probably know a great deal more about babies than I do, but I know that she'd really like to have me there. Getting used to being parents is something you both do together, I think. In agreeing to let me do what I've always dreamed of, Elaine has given me something truly special. I'm not sure I'll ever be able to repay her. The only thing I can do is make the sacrifice worthwhile.

When we players speak about sacrifice, we don't just mean for ourselves. We mean the sacrifices made by those around us, who support us and push us on, who give things up so that we can do the job we love. I may have done the heavy lifting, the training sessions and the eating regime, the early mornings in the gym and the sleepless nights wondering about the next match, but it's my family and Elaine who have made that possible. Having Dad here in Australia has been special, as has meeting his family who live in Australia, as well as cousins I've never met before, and I'm so glad that they were in the Melbourne Cricket Ground to see the match.

I was once a young boy in my Lions shirt, watching the team play on the other side of the world, dreaming about being one of them. Now, little boys and girls are watching me and my teammates and wanting to be like us. Things have come full circle in my life, and that feels good. But I haven't done it alone. Legendary athlete Michael Jordan said: 'One thing I believe to the fullest is that if you think and achieve as a team, the individual accolades will take care of themselves. Talent wins games, but teamwork and intelligence win championships.' We have achieved everything we have because we've done it together. That's what I will take away from this tour.

CHAPTER 13

WHAT HAPPENS AFTER

'If I gave one piece of advice to a player retiring tomorrow, I'd say: "When you wake up, have something to do. Something, anything. It doesn't matter what. Anything that helps you feel useful. Because the worst thing is the void. "'

Jorge Valdano, Argentinian footballer and former manager of Real Madrid

My tattoos tell the story of my life. When I was younger, I often used to tell Mum that one day, when I was rich and famous, I'd take her to Rome. Why Rome, I don't know, but it became a running story between the two of us, a daydream that we both shared. That's why my first tattoo was of one of the statues on the famous bridge across the Tiber that leads to the Castel Sant'Angelo, complete with Mum's name. I got it done in Skin City in Dublin and it's a reminder to me never to take what I've got for granted and to make the very best out of the life I've been given. I know that's what Mum would want for me.

Paddy Fintan in Donegal has become a good friend of mine, which is fortunate as he spent about sixteen hours tattooing my right forearm after the 2023 World Cup. He lives way up in Carndonagh, on Malin Head, but he's such a brilliant tattoo artist that he has a steady stream of clients, including some of my teammates. It's great fun to sit in his shop and see people 'wandering by' for a look. Paddy says that I like some 'dark and crazy' tattoos, but really it's the aesthetic that appeals to me. I'll get an idea in my head for a tattoo, based maybe on an image I've seen, and I'll sketch it out so I can see how it looks on paper. Then I'll leave it for a while to see if I like it. If it's a keeper, I'll get in touch with Paddy.

I have a Viking-themed tattoo on my left leg, for example, because I became a bit obsessed with the TV show *The Vikings* and because I've always loved the Viking imagery of the Swedish metal band Amon Amarth. I read quite a lot of Norse mythology at one point and got really into them. I'm not a religious person, but I love the stories of the Norse gods and feel that there's a lot to the imagery and storytelling. I love Odin, the father of everything, and the way he removed an eye so he could see the world as it really was. Thor is another favourite, and I love the way he could make the weather do anything, from storms to thunder, to reflect his hot-tempered personality.

I also like the Japanese aesthetic: it's really restrained and so different from the Norse mythology, which is why I have a Japanese-style tattoo on my right leg. And before the last Lions game in Sydney I went with Finlay Bealham and Will Stuart to get a lion tattoo with my cap number, 876, underneath. The lion looks remarkably like Finlay. Elaine doesn't love tattoos in general, but she's come to accept mine, as long as I don't go near my neck or my face. Sometimes she'll think a new one is really quite nice. Some of my friends might joke, 'Imagine what they'll look like when you're fifty!', but I love them.

Being on the Lions team in Australia was everything I'd worked for, the summit of my own Everest. Before the final game in Sydney, Faz had organised for Irish boxing legend Katie Taylor to give us a team talk. Her inspirational words 'Prepare to win by skill, but be ready to win by will' rang in our ears as we took to the rain-sodden pitch. The Australian winter was producing torrential rain and storms, and the Accor stadium didn't have a roof. The dreadful conditions meant that ball handling would be difficult and our kicking game would be key.

I was starting, and up against Taniela Tupou, also known as the 'Tongan Thor', and Will Skelton, who I knew from La Rochelle. Together they weighed about 285kg, and were aggressive in the ruck from the off. The Wallabies got their first try after eight minutes with a Dylan Pietsch dive, followed by a Tom Lynagh penalty at 33 minutes. We were playing catch-up, and the game had turned into a war of attrition, with plenty of shithousery.

Maro Itoje went off with a HIA, as did Lynagh. At half time Dan Sheehan gave a speech warning us that we needed to cut the errors and keep our discipline, but were barely back on the pitch when James Ryan got a knee to the head from Skelton, knocking him out. I saw red and went for Skelton, which earned me a penalty. Thankfully by the time the medics had James on the stretcher he was able to give a thumbs up.

In the meantime the storm continued to rage overhead and the ref informed us that we needed to head to the dressing rooms as there was a lightning warning in place. Thirty-five frustrating minutes later play had resumed, but I'd been replaced by Eilis Genge and my Lions playing time was over. The Wallabies got another try before Jac Morgan responded with one for us and Finn Russell converted, with Tate McDermott and Will Stuart also swapping tries. The score finished up 22-12.

The game was a proper battle, but we had won the war. By the time Maro lifted the silver trophy the smile was back on my face. It was a bittersweet moment too though, as we all knew that we'd soon be back on a plane to our normal lives, and missing the huge connection we'd all enjoyed over the past two months. As Faz told the media, 'This has been the time of our lives and that sounds dramatic, but it's the truth.'

Finishing up with the Lions is also a solid reminder that this game won't last forever.

Ask any rugby player about the end of their career and they won't really want to think about it. None of us wants to get to the end of the playing road, and yet sooner or later we do. All the greats become once-greats and accepting that is a process that I know I'll have to go through at the end of my playing career. There's a great photo of Roger Federer and Rafael Nadal sitting beside each other after Federer's final match, both of them in tears at the prospect of their time in tennis ending. To me, this sums up the feeling that nothing lasts for ever, even the sport I love, so I know that I need to prepare for the next phase of my life. Tough, when I've been involved with the game for almost my whole life.

Does it keep me awake at night? Sometimes. I have read various stories about sports people struggling in retirement, so I know that I'll have to be mindful of 'the void', as Jorge Valdano says. He should know, having had a career as both footballer and manager. He told the BBC, 'Footballers never talk about the end of their careers, for the same reason human beings don't talk about death: it frightens them.' He's got a point. Something that was once your whole identity is now gone. For some people, it might feel as if they've disappeared.

I can imagine that I'll have to find a new identity both in and outside rugby.

I'm trying to put as much in place as I can to make the transition easier while continuing to enjoy the present. It's different for every player, I think. I know that some people worry about finance after playing; others worry about losing the excitement of the game, that big adrenaline rush that comes with a win. I know I'll miss that, but I can't see myself trekking to the North Pole or rowing across the Atlantic in search of it … mowing the lawn is more my style. But you never know. However, I was struck by what Brendan Cannon, the former Wallaby, had to say about retirement: '[People] want to talk to you about what you used to be, and all you want to focus on is what you want to become.' I can imagine that I'll feel the sting when people come up to me wanting to share a special moment in my sporting career with me, when I have the rest of my life in front of me.

As to what I'll do, an office is probably not for me, so I'd ideally like to continue working in the training, strength and fitness area, which is why setting up a gym is the perfect next step. I think it's something I'd be good at, not just because I do it but because I know how important exercise is to mental health. After all, it was crucial to me regaining my own sense of self and wellbeing when

I was a teenager. It's also been hugely beneficial to me in managing my ADHD, giving my mind something to really zone in on. So I've been taking steps in that direction with a friend, doing a qualification in the practical side of things. A lot of the lads are doing extra qualifications while they're actively playing so that they're ready to jump in when the time comes.

Having said that, modern sport tends to be all or nothing, in that as a sportsperson your schedule is jam-packed when you're actively playing, now more than ever, so when that ends, there's definitely a time of transition. However, I think if you know that you will be hanging up your boots in the not-too-distant future, this gives you some control over the outcome. My friend and teammate Conor Murray said on his retirement after the Six Nations: 'I've been lucky and grateful to be part of this Irish set-up. It's sad, it'll be emotional but I've seen so many players not get to end it on their terms, career cut short. The fact I get to do it on my own terms when I'm fit and healthy is something very few people get to do, so I'm very grateful.' I think that's really important. I am well aware of the fact that it'll all end some day and this gives me the added impetus to think, *Right, while I'm in this I'll have a blast.* And when it's done, I won't be able to say that I didn't give it my best shot. I don't want to have any regrets.

I know that I'll probably struggle with the lack of organised time, though. This has helped me so much and I know that I'll have to find my own routines and schedules instead. I'm used to being told what to do and where and when to do it, so having to make my own decisions will be interesting. I think this will take time.

But what about the benefits of retirement? Well, I look forward to having my weekends back and to spending time with my family. The modern playing schedule is pretty full-on, with just a few weeks off a year, and it will be great to have the luxury of time. I know I'll find it hard to manage in some ways because scheduling keeps me focused, but I'm confident that my family will keep me occupied and grounded. I really look forward to spending time with Elaine and Max and hopefully a growing family. I want to spend more time with Dad and to persuade him to retire! My whole family, and particularly Elaine, have made so many sacrifices to allow me to do this job, so it'll be great to be able to repay them, even if in only a small way.

I also look forward to continuing my work with the Irish Cancer Society, because it's my way of staying connected to Mum, but also because they do so much to help those suffering from cancer and their families. I even had my head shaved live on *The Late Late Show* to raise funds for the charity in 2022. I remember it well because everyone in the audience was masked up, so when I looked out, all I could see was row upon row of face masks. When Elaine was asked what she thought about my newly shaven head, she wasn't all that sure. At the time, my bleached-blond mullet was my trademark, but it was good to lose it for such a great cause.

In fact, talking of face masks, I remember that I helped them design the Irish Cancer Society face mask during Covid and even provided drawings for the mask. They sold in lots of places around the world and raised some money. I remember being out with Elaine doing some Christmas shopping in 2020 and I saw a few people wearing them. The fact that people had my drawings on their faces was weird, but brilliant. It was a real privilege to help raise some funds for them because cancer impacts so many of us. As an ambassador with the Irish Cancer Society, I want to use my status to benefit others and hopefully to make other people's lives a bit better. What I do is small compared with the incredible work the volunteers and staff do there, but even in a small way, I want to help to raise awareness and boost campaigns.

I'm also involved with Movember, which has become such a great way of opening up the conversation around men's mental and physical health. It started off as a men's cancer charity, a place where men could talk about what they were going through with prostate cancer, but over time it's developed into a charity that supports men's mental health as well, with over a thousand separate programmes in operation. Mack Hansen and I are both ambassadors and have both spoken out about our stories and what helped us. It's great to know that the subject of men's mental health is no longer taboo and that men can talk more openly about their feelings. You can look incredibly strong on the outside and people don't know what's going on behind the scenes.

One of my favourite places to chat is in my friend Ben Condron's Choppers Barbers. Not only is he responsible for some of my iconic cuts, such as the mullet, he's also a great guy to chat to. He understands the importance of mental health and the power of the barber's as an easy place for men to have a conversation. You're not eyeballing each other or face to face, so you can casually talk about all kinds of things. You'd be amazed at the deep conversations that take place in Ben's.

It was an easy decision to get behind the Tackle Your Feelings initiative when I was asked. It's especially aimed at younger people in schools, and that means a lot to me. I know what it's like to be isolated and lonely during the most challenging years of life, and if I can share my experiences, that might help someone else. They have an app too that provides some tools that can help. Something that might work for one person might not work for someone else, but there'll be something there that can get a young person started on the right path.

A lot of people have asked me what it'll be like for me physically, because so much of my identity is about my build. It's a good question. I'll keep up the training, I know, because I love the way it makes me feel. I love what it does for my mind, I love what it does for my body. I even train on holiday … Maybe Elaine would be happy to be able to go and see museums and travel without me having to train before we step out the door, but to me it's an essential part of my day. I don't think I'll lose that.

When I was a kid, training got me through a lot because I was able to use it to physically see improvements, whether it was for myself or for my rugby. I suppose it was something I could control when things seemed out of control. Now, I've come to rely on that discipline. I track everything I eat on apps and I like knowing that I'm getting what I need. It's about accountability to myself. Training has always been a huge part of my life and it'll continue to be so. It has such great health and longevity benefits. I want to be in the best shape I can be for my family. However, I am aware of the problems that former sportsmen and women can face physically in later life. Things like arthritis, weight gain, even brain injury. The game is so much safer now than it was, but it's also physically demanding. I know that answering those demands might cause me some difficulties down the line, and this does worry me sometimes. I can't let it hold me back in the present, though, because otherwise I couldn't do my job. And the management are really good at looking after us nowadays.

I was always really competitive with my dad. I was always trying to arm wrestle him and to climb hills faster than him. I know I'll be competitive with Max, but I hope to set the right kind of example as a dad also. I've been told that when it comes to parenting, kids actually follow 'Do what I do, not what I say.' I can tell Max all I want to eat his vegetables, to be polite and respectful of others and to be kind, but I know that I need to model that in my own life so that he has an example to follow. I also want to share a love of just moving with him. He doesn't have to be a rugby player, or to love training as I do: but I think it's so important that he takes exercise and spends time outdoors. I know how beneficial that is to my mental health as well as to my body.

Looking into the future is never easy when you're a professional sportsperson. I know that many of them find the transition a challenge. But I've met challenges before, and faced them, and overcome them, so I know I'll face this one too – and with the help of my loved ones, I'll come out the other side. For now, I'll keep going as long as I can. The obstacle is the way.

ACKNOWLEDGEMENTS

Writing this book has been one of the most challenging and rewarding journeys of my life. It
wouldn't have been possible without the support, guidance
and belief of so many incredible people.

First and foremost, to my wife Elaine – thank you
for being the constant in my life, for your love, strength
and endless support. You helped me see that by sharing
my struggles, I could help others who might be silently
fighting their own. This book exists because you believed
in its purpose – and in me. You are an amazing partner and
a wonderful mother to our son, and I'm grateful for you
every single day.

To my parents – my mum Wendy, who is no longer

with us but whose presence I still feel and cherish – and especially my dad, who dedicated so much to giving me the best opportunity to be the best version of myself. Your sacrifices laid the foundation for everything I've achieved.

To my sisters, Erica and Leigh – thank you for your love, your encouragement and for always being in my corner.

To my team at Navy Blue, especially Niall Woods, Gemma Kenny and Jordi Murphy – your guidance, belief in me and tireless work behind the scenes have made a huge difference in my career, both on and off the pitch.

Thank you to Deirdre Nolan, publishing director at Eriu, your support and belief in the book means everything. Thank you also to Lisa Gilmour, assistant editor at Eriu. Big thanks to the Gill Hess team: Simon Hess, Declan Heeney, Helen McKean and Jacq Murphy, for your expertise. To the marketing and publicity team in Bonnier Books UK, thank you.

To my friends and teammates – thank you for the laughter, the loyalty and the honest conversations. Whether it was on the training field, during the toughest matches, or in the quiet moments off the pitch, your presence has meant more than you know. You've helped shape the man and player I've become.

And finally, to Alison Walsh and Richie Sadlier – thank you for your patience, your insight and for sitting with me through countless hours of conversation to help bring this story to life. Your help has been invaluable in shaping this book into something I can be proud of.

This story is not just mine – it belongs to everyone who walked with me through the darkest times and helped me come out stronger on the other side.

PICTURE CREDITS

First section

All images courtesy of the Porter family, with the exception of Page 3: (*bottom*) Celtic League Rugby Leinster 26/11/2004: Mascots with Leo Cullen and Des Dillon © INPHO/Billy Stickland

Second section

Page one: (*top*) Andrew Porter of Leinster is tackled by Alberto De Marchi and Ornel Gega, of Treviso during the Guinness PRO12 Round 1 match between Leinster and Treviso at the RDS Arena in Ballsbridge, Dublin © Getty Images/Stephen McCarthy; (*bottom*) Ireland's James Ryan, left, and Andrew Porter following their international debut in the international match between Ireland and USA at the Red Bull Arena in Harrison, New Jersey, USA © Getty Images/Ramsey Cardy

Page two: (*top*) Andrew Porter celebrates with the Triple Crown and Six Nations Championship trophies after the NatWest Six Nations Rugby Championship match between England and Ireland at Twickenham Stadium in London, England © Getty Images/Brendan Moran; (*bottom*) Andrew Porter of Ireland is tackled by Owen Farrell, left, and Manu Tuilagi of England during the Guinness Six Nations Rugby Championship match between Ireland and England at Aviva Stadium in Dublin © Getty Images/Ramsey Cardy

Page three: (*top*) Andrew Porter of Leinster in action in the maul during the Leinster vs Scarlets, United Rugby Championship match at RDS Arena on 16 October 2021 in Dublin, Ireland © Getty Images/Tim Clayton/Corbis; (*bottom*) © Leinster players, from left, Rory O'Loughlin, Andrew Porter, Garry Ringrose and James Tracy with the Guinness PRO14 trophy following the Guinness PRO14 Final match between Leinster and Ulster at the empty Aviva Stadium in Dublin © Getty Images/Ramsey Cardy

Page four: (*top*) Andrew Porter of Ireland scores a try during the International Test match between the New Zealand All Blacks and Ireland at Forsyth Barr Stadium on 9 July 2022 in Dunedin, New Zealand © Getty Images/Hagin Hopkins; (*bottom*) Andrew Porter of Ireland is consoled by his wife Elaine after his side's defeat in the 2023 Rugby World Cup quarter-final match between Ireland and New Zealand at the Stade de France in Paris, France © Getty Images/Brendan Moran

Page five: (*top*) Qatar Airways 2025 British and Irish Lions Tour to Australia First Test, Suncorp Stadium, Australia: Wallabies vs British and Irish Lions 19 July 2025 © Inpho/Dan Sheridan; (*bottom*) 2025 British and Irish Lions Tour to Australia Third Test, Accor Stadium, Sydney, Australia 2/8/2025, Lion's players celebrate after the match in the dressing room with the Qatar Airways series trophy © INPHO/Dan Sheridan

Page six: (*top*) Andrew Porter opens up about mental health as part of the Tackle Your Feelings campaign, encouraging open conversations and emotional resilience © Tackle Your Feelings/Dan Sheridan; (*middle*) Andrew Porter joins forces with Movember to champion men's health – raising awareness for prostate cancer, testicular cancer and mental well-being through powerful storytelling and community engagement © Movember/Greg Byrne; (*bottom*) 7 December 2020. Irish Rugby star and Irish Cancer Society Ambassador Andrew Porter pictured wearing one of the face masks he designed for the Irish Cancer Society © Leon Farrell/Photocall Ireland

Page seven: Images courtesy of the Porter family

Page eight: (*top*) Image courtesy of the Porter Family; (*bottom*) BKT United Rugby Championship Grand Final, Croke Park, Dublin 14 June 2025 Leinster vs Vodacom Bulls: Leinster's Andrew Porter celebrates with champagne in the dressing room after the game © INPHO/Ben Brady

INDEX